W9-BGH-646

Community Work and Social Work

LIBRARY OF SOCIAL WORK

GENERAL EDITOR : NOEL TIMMS

Professor of Applied Social Studies
University of Bradford

Community Work and Social Work

Peter Baldock

Community Worker
Sheffield Family and Community Services Department

London and Boston

Routledge & Kegan Paul

First published in 1974
by Routledge & Kegan Paul Ltd
Broadway House, 68-74 Carter Lane,
London EC4V 5EL and
9 Park Street,
Boston, Mass. 02108, USA
Set in 10 point Pilgrim on 12 point body
and printed in Great Britain by
Northumberland Press Limited, Gateshead
© Peter Baldock 1974
ISBN 0 7100 80263 (c)
      0 7100 80271 (p)

General editor's introduction

The Library of Social Work was originally designed to make a contribution to the recent significant expansion in social work education. Not only were increasing numbers of students training for social work, but the changing demands of the work and widening view of its theoretical bases were producing considerable changes in the basic curriculum of social work education. In this situation a library of short texts intended to introduce a subject, to assess its relevance for social work, and to guide further reading had a distinctive contribution to make. The continuing success of the Library of Social Work shows that this contribution is still highly valued.

The Library of Social Work will, therefore, continue to produce short introductory texts, but it will also enlarge its range to include the longer, more sustained treatment of subjects relevant to social work. Monographs reporting research, collections of papers, the more detailed and substantial explanation of the knowledge base of social work, could all be encompassed within this wider definition of the scope of the Library of Social Work.

In moments of inattention it seems perhaps that community work has come among us somewhat suddenly. Yet, as Peter Baldock shows in his first chapter, community work has developed through a number of phases. The relationship between the Charity Organisation Society (or at least a rather forgotten element in its work) and the present possible view of community work as a specific radical social movement is not simply one of contradiction. Community work has a twofold interest for social workers in general.

First, as we have just seen, community work is part of the history of social work. Second, throughout its development it has posed, implicitly or explicitly, boundary questions of considerable significance. The relationship between community work and casework is discussed in some detail in chapter six of this book, but as the author discusses the Principles, Values and Objectives in Community Work, and the various phases through which Community Groups may progress new light is cast on similarities and differences. We shall not in future be able to assume rather casually that social work is, like Gaul, fixedly divided into three parts—casework, groupwork, and community work.

It is not easy to feel confident that we know what 'community work' is or how it may relate to aspects or methods of social work about which we may feel more sure—at least until we examine them in some critical detail. Previous attempts at clarifying community work have suffered from two main shortcomings: they have been addressed to wide, unspecified audiences and frequently they have been couched in a highly theoretical or rhetorical mode. The present work has a particular audience in mind. Community work is described for the primary benefit of social workers 'whose work comes mainly through the referral of individuals and families with particular problems'. Of course, as the author suggests, this does not render the book superfluous for others who might be interested in community work—youth leaders, clergy and so on. It is simply a focus for picking out important aspects. Similarly, the author is clearly aware of the theoretical and ideological problems involved in community work, but this introduction aims at enlarging an understanding of community work activity through clear and simple practical description of the range of work undertaken and of skill deployed. This study does not get lost in the stratosphere of general values, though values are not neglected.

Contents

CONTENTS

Acknowledgments

Between 1971 and 1974 I was Student Unit Supervisor at the Manchester and Salford Council of Social Service (now the Manchester Council of Voluntary Service). There is no better way of learning about something than trying to teach others and I am grateful to the tutors and students from social work courses with whom I worked at that time for the discussions that formed the starting point for this book.

I also wish to acknowledge the assistance of Professor Noel Timms in the preparation of this book.

Introduction

The last few years have seen a massive expansion in community work in this country, much of it taking place within the new Social Services Departments. Social workers are being asked to work with community workers as colleagues and to face up to the 'challenge of community work'. Yet, in spite of text-book references to community work as the 'third method of social work' (along with casework and group work), few social workers in this country have any clear conception of who the community workers are, how they are trained or who employs them, what skills they have or how they use them.

The object of this book is to introduce community work, but not to set it in the overall context of social policy or social change. Nor is this a text book telling the reader how to do community work, though some discussion of methods is inevitable. The book merely aims to give as clear a picture as possible of what it is.

It is also a book aimed at a particular audience. It would be possible to write such an introduction for planners, youth workers, clergymen or members of some other profession. There would be a good deal of overlap between the contents of this book and of a similar book addressed to a different audience. But there would also be differences of approach as well as of content. This book is intended for social caseworkers. I deliberately avoid the use of the wider term 'social worker'. I have in mind the reader whose work comes mainly through the referral of individuals and families with particular problems and who wants to know how he should relate to community workers and how he can employ some community work skills in his main task and who, in order to do this, needs first of all to have a clearer picture of what community work is.

Inevitably a book of this brevity will have gaps. There are two in particular that I regret. Although community workers operating in rural situations have contributed considerably to theory and practice in this country and abroad, I scarcely refer to them. Neither is there any consideration of the particular situations affecting the relationship of community work to social work in Scotland and Northern Ireland. Both these omissions are due simply to my own ignorance.

'Community work' is a term sufficiently precise to be meaningful, but not so precise as to ensure that any two self-styled community workers will agree even on what is to be called 'community work', let alone on methods or principles. The term is used in this book to refer to a number of related, but varying, activities conducted by people with a wide range of values. Community work seems to me neither to be nor to be prospectively a profession or a specific social movement. It is, in other words, something of a mess. But it is also important and interesting. I hope that this book will reflect the latter two qualities rather than the first.

I

What community work is

The development of community work

It is arbitrary, but convenient, to divide the history of community work in this country into four overlapping phases.

The first phase lasted from the 1880s to the 1920s and was one in which community work was merely an aspect of social work.

The second lasted from the 1920s to the 1950s and marked the emergence of a separate range of skills and concerns. It was closely associated with the increasing part played by central and local government in urban development and its focal point was the Community Association movement.

The third phase was in part a reaction against the 'neighbourhood/community idea' (Dennis, 1958) which had provided the ideological basis for the second phase. It saw the emergence of a group of people who sought a professional identity as community workers either within or separate from the social work profession and its culminating point was the publication of *Community Work and Social Change* (*Gulbenkian Study Group*, 1968), a highly influential document which helped to bring about the expansion in the number of community work posts in the late 1960s and early 1970s.

The fourth phase saw the massive expansion in the number of community workers. It was marked by an increasing involvement in community action and a questioning of the concepts of non-directive methods, consensus strategies and professionalism that had been developed by the academics and fieldworkers in the third phase. It was in this most recent phase that the question of the relationship of community work to social work became more controversial and difficult on both sides.

The first phase and the emergence of a social work profession

At one time what we might now call 'community work' formed an important part of what we might now call 'social work'.

The basic facts about the Charity Organisation Society are already well known to students of social casework. What is, perhaps, less stressed in the text books is that not only did the COS lay the foundations for casework in this country, but that the very attempt to organise charity involved the co-ordination of the work of many people in a way reminiscent of some types of community work today. Even more clearly an early instance of community work was the formation of the National Council of Social Service in 1919 and of many local Councils of Social Service in the years that followed. Councils of Social Service were intended to be means of co-ordinating the work of voluntary agencies. In the event it proved impossible to reconcile real co-ordination with the highly valued independence of the agencies. In any case voluntary agencies began to play a more subsidiary role as the welfare state was established. But some forms of liaison were possible. In particular, Councils of Social Service became a medium through which new experiments in social work could be launched, and many of these were in club work and the recreational field. Such work had been pioneered earlier by the Settlements which were set up in working-class areas of the major cities in the thirty years before the First World War. The Settlements were buildings in which university students and graduates resided in order to be able to offer leadership to their adopted working-class neighbours in a variety of social and recreational activities. The COS, the Settlements and the Councils of Social Service formed the most important elements in social work in this country fifty years ago and (in so far as the modern forms are identifiable in the activities in which they engaged) they were as much community work as casework agencies.

Of course, a good deal of their work is now criticised in ways that echo the socialists of their time. When not harsh it was often paternalistic. The casework revolution, by which I mean the increasing use of material from theoretical psychology to understand clients' behaviour, was to a large extent a reaction against the social work establishment dominated by a few figures in the COS, the NCSS and the Settlements. It involved a rejection of the assumption of class superiority that had informed much of the thinking of the social work pioneers. In training in particular it involved an attempt to develop natural sympathy in workers who might otherwise have remained mere bureaucrats. In this sense the casework revolution was a liberating process that involved the absorption of new knowledge and approaches where they were desperately needed.

This was not the only effect. Casework also helped to give social work a professional status. 'Professionalism' is sometimes spoken of in social work circles as though it were a moral virtue. It is more accurate to speak of it as a social movement. It is a development which over the last hundred years has done much to secure a position of relatively high status for those who could not remain capitalists in a period of increasing monopolisation and would have resented being made obvious proletarians. Social workers remain middle-class people (if only by naturalisation through the education system) who are dealing with clients who are largely of lower status than themselves. Inevitably a strong class element remains in the relationship. This is evidenced by frequent difficulties in communication between clients and workers and by conflicts of loyalty workers sometimes feel as between their clients and their employers. It is argued by many within the social work profession itself that the mere fact of dealing with individual problems tends to suggest that the problems lie with the individuals when in fact they lie with the structural relationships of a class society.

Gradually it has been realised that the combination of welfare state provision and counselling services has not been enough to rid the country of poverty and distress. With this has come an increasing appreciation of our apparent inability to control urban development for the good of all. There has been a reaction against casework in the sense both of dealing with individual clients separately and of dealing with them in the light of psychoanalytic theory. While only a minority has taken this reaction all the way, most would accept the need for additional models for working with those who have social problems. Hence the recent interest among social workers in community work.

The second phase and the neighbourhood/community idea

This is not the first time there has been a movement of this sort. A similar move got under way in 1928 when the New Estates Committee of the National Council of Social Service—later the National Federation of Community Associations—was formed. Many of the moves sponsored by community workers in the 1930s, 1940s and early 1950s bore, however, the same stamp of conservative reaction against modern urban society as had the earlier Settlement movement. The attitude that lay behind this work was well summarised by the American sociologist and community organisation theorist Robert Park. 'We are seeking,' he wrote, 'to do, through the medium of our local community organisations, such things as will get action and interest for the little world of the locality. We are encouraging a new parochialism, seeking to initiate a movement that will run counter to the current romanticism with its eye always on the horizon, one which will recognise limits and work within them. Our problem is to encourage men to seek God in their own villages and to see the social problem in their own neighbourhood' (Park, 1952, p. 72). Together with this new parochialism went an insistence in this country that localities needed 'social balance'. It was said that there should be a middle-class minority in each neighbourhood that could assume the leadership in local affairs (White, 1950). In brief, there was an attempt to build a static, hierarchical society of narrow perspectives that was assumed to be similar to the community of the medieval village.

Inevitably the attempt was a failure. Community Associations, while often doing a useful job, were not the organised forms of local social systems, but groups pursuing particular interests (Twelvetrees, 1971). In the absence of actual coercion, it proved impossible for the most part to persuade middle-class people to live in working-class neighbourhoods and offer them 'leadership'. The second wave of community work was an ideological response to the creation of massive new residential areas in the inter-war period and a reflection of the general anxiety to return to what was taken for normality after the social crisis of the 1930s and the Second World War. It ran itself into the ground.

The third phase and the stress on a professional, consensus approach

From the middle 1960s onwards there were new developments in community work (foreshadowed by pioneer work in the London and Liverpool Councils of Social Service in the 1950s) which did not depend on a nostalgic rejection of the present, though they did stem from an appreciation of deficiencies in the existing urban situation. There were moves within education and social work, and later planning and other professions, to open up their areas of activity and responsibility in ways that would take effective note of new knowledge in the social sciences and failures in existing practice.

Reacting against the tendency to regard the Community Association structure as a universally applicable blueprint, many workers involved in this third phase were very much influenced by Batten's stress on the principle that non-directive methods were preferable in many circumstances (Batten, 1967). There was also an increasing stress on professionalism (Thomason, 1969). Both these features were evident in the work of Ilys Booker, a well-known fieldworker whose approach was characterised by a consensus strategy and who sought to advance the professionalism of community work by subjecting her own work to critical evaluation. (See especially Mitton and Morrison, 1972, but also Booker, 1960, 1962, and Goetschius, 1969.)

Some of the ideas developed in this third phase were taken up in chapter 16 of the Seebohm Report (Seebohm, 1968). This says that the proposed Social Services Departments should not merely concentrate on establishing effective casework and subsidiary services. The freedom from the constraints of existing and institutionalised specialisms and the increasing stress on area organisation should make possible a new relationship between the catchment areas of departments and their workers. The committee saw this happening in two major ways. The departments should encourage, promote and support voluntary effort. This was seen, not merely as adding to resources, but as a means of involving the public more extensively in social services. The second approach concerned what the report called 'the need for the personal social services to engage in this extremely difficult and complex task of assisting and encouraging the development of community identity and mutual aid, particularly in areas characterised by rapid population turnover, high delinquency, child deprivation and mental illness rates and other indices of social pathology'. This need arose because 'social work with individuals alone is bound to be of limited effect in an area where the community environment itself is a major impediment to healthy individual development' (Para. 477). The report went on to say that: 'A sense of community (and all that implies) may need to be promoted among people for whom it does not exist, whilst in recognisable communities effort may be needed to preserve and strengthen common identity and activity' (Para. 482).

There are many criticisms to be made of chapter 16 of the

Seebohm Report. It does not distinguish sufficiently between different types of volunteer and the sort of work they can be expected to undertake. In the paragraphs dealing with areas of high deprivation it fails entirely to come to grips with the issue of whether community work in such areas that focused on 'community identity' might not impede, or at least fail to contribute to, the development of collective action to tackle more fundamental problems that lie behind 'indices of social pathology'. But chapter 16 was highly influential and many of the new Social Services Departments have appointed workers at various levels with a dual responsibility for volunteer organisation and something loosely labelled 'community development'.

It was not just social work that was involved in the new interest in community work. Education was another profession with an evident interest. Community centres, for example, had long been the responsibility of Local Education Authorities. The year after Seebohm saw the production of another influential official document, *Youth and Community Work in the 1970s* (Youth Service Development Council, 1969), which insisted on the need for a greater involvement by the youth service in work with young people outside clubs and work with the adults concerned with young people.

But the most influential document was an unofficial one which goes under the common name of the 'Gulbenkian Report' (Gulbenkian Study Group, 1968). In 1965 the Gulbenkian Foundation, a leading charitable trust, gave money for an investigation of community work by a small study group consisting of practitioners and interested academics. The group produced its report entitled *Community Work and Social Change* in the same year as the Seebohm Committee. Although Dame Eileen Younghusband was the chairman, the group had adult education as well as social work as a significant reference point. The object of the working party was to make proposals on training and these take up the greater part of the report. But the question was: training for what? And the first 83 pages of the report are taken up with a discursive definition of community work.

The term 'community work' was, in fact, to a large extent established in common usage by the working party, other terms having been widely used until that time. They claimed to find a common element in the work of a large number of people in that they were all 'concerned with affecting the course of social change through the two processes of analysing social situations and forming relationships with different groups to bring about some desirable change' (p. 4).

The group defined three main types of work that could be defined in these terms and proposed that the term 'community work' be used for all three of them.

The first was the work of a small, but increasing, number of people who were, so to speak, counsellors to small community groups, such as Tenants' Associations and Pre-School Play Groups. Sometimes these people were employed to work in single urban neighbourhoods or restricted rural areas. Sometimes they were based on central offices—of local authority departments, voluntary organisations or federations of community groups—and offered their help to a wide number of groups in different areas. Their role was, like that of the caseworker with his client, to help people to express their needs and take appropriate (in this case collective) action to meet them, with the additional resource of any hard information or other help that the worker was able to offer. Many such workers had previously worked in developing countries, using what were known as 'community development' techniques in supporting local self-help groups.

The second type of work was that of seeking to encourage greater liaison between different agencies and groups either in an open-ended way or in order to promote new joint projects. This had always been a central task of, for example, General Secretaries of Councils of Social Service.

The third type of work was that of research and development in all areas of social welfare. This went hand in hand with a stress on social or community planning among those in the planning profession and suggestions in the *Report of the Committee on Public Participation in Planning* that the views and interests of ordinary citizens should be taken into greater consideration in the formulation of plans (Skeffington, 1969).

Of course, these types of work were not seen as strictly separate. To take one example, the team in the Social Development Office of a New Town Development Corporation might be 1. helping residents to form groups to tackle immediate problems and to help in the settling-in process, 2. helping various agencies in the new town to co-operate effectively, and 3. advising other departments of the Development Corporation on social needs in the new town.

What is interesting (and this, as much as the lack of emphasis on the role of social work in community work, was a reflection of the composition of the Gulbenkian Group) is that the working party thought in both large- and small-scale terms. That is to say that they might not have included under the heading of 'community work' much that forms part of the second type of work or anything that forms part of the third. In practice the term 'community worker' itself has tended to be used normally to refer to those working with small neighbourhood or special interest groups. A recent publication *Current Issues in Community Work* (Community Work Group, 1973) labels the first of the three types of work outlined in the Gulbenkian Report as 'community (field) work'. This is the field with which this book will be mainly concerned, if only because it is the most important growth point.

The three-part classification proposed in the Gulbenkian Report offers one way of looking at community work. Another is to look at present activity as it relates to different professional backgrounds.

Probably a majority of community workers is employed in what are essentially social work agencies, though it appears from the (pretty unreliable) figures available that less than a fifth of community workers in the country have social work qualifications. Those who in some sense see their work in relation to social work are concerned with five main areas. The first is that of promoting inter-agency liaison. The second is that of organising volunteers. A third field is the new, expanding one of play leadership and organisation. A fourth is the more established one of club work with the physically and mentally handicapped. A fifth is in work with 'clients' organisations', such as Claimants' Unions and Tenants' Associations.

Some community workers would dispute the suggestion that all these forms of activity come under the heading of community work and, in particular, would want to exclude work with groups of people having specific problems when these groups are promoted by Social Services Departments. It seems to me that the deciding point is the approach adopted. If the worker is attempting to promote self-directed, collective activity by a group, such as the physically handicapped, then it is legitimate to call this community work. If he is merely providing a service, such as recreation facilities, for a client group, then it is not. On the other hand, many Social Services Departments appear to stretch the use of the term 'community work' too far, probably because it became such a 'hooray' term in the years after 1968. To describe the routine organisation of day or foster care as 'community work' is to reveal muddled thinking. (Of course, the use or non-use of the term 'community work' in such situations is a matter of the accurate use of language, not of bestowing or withholding approval.)

Probably the longest established group of community workers are those whose professional ties are with education. Community centres provided by Local Education Authorities have already been mentioned. There are interesting attempts in Liverpool, Sheffield and elsewhere to make adult education more relevant to the working class by relating it to the needs that working-class organisations often have of greater knowledge of local and national structures and by abandoning the formal lecture in the classroom as the standard method of teaching (Clyne, 1974). In the youth service, inside and outside clubs and centres, there is greater emphasis on the need for the worker to promote self-directed activity by young people rather than attempting to impose a rigid club discipline.

A third type of work is in community relations. Most towns and cities now have Community Relations Councils. These are voluntary bodies working on a basis laid down by the 1968 Race Relations Act (though some of them are derived from agencies that were established before the Act). They are not responsible for the formal reconciliation procedures established by the Act, but are supposed to take a greater initiative. Their role is to assist racial minorities to live a satisfactory life in this country. Much of their work is often casework with black people or straight education (for example, assisting in 'civics' teaching in schools). But they also engage in helping relationships with ethnic organisations, inter-racial bodies and various agencies, particularly major local authority departments, which have a great deal of influence over the opportunities offered to black people in this country.

A fourth group consists of those concerned with issues in urban development and this is one of the most complex to discuss because it is the one least concerned with any one existing professional establishment, although an increasing number of radical planners are becoming involved in community work.

A number of agencies concerned with housing and planning are considering the employment of, or already employ, specialists in community work. The Social Development sections of New Town Development Corporations have already been mentioned. Some Housing Departments and Housing Associations employ arrivals officers who work on new estates or blocks for the first couple of years, helping the first residents to settle in such areas. Others employ workers to deal with tenants' halls built by them under the 1919 Housing Act. The old London County Council preferred to work through the London Council of Social Service to a large extent for this sort of work, but still provided a good deal of the necessary money. There was a proposal from the Skeffington Committee that local authorities should employ workers within Planning Departments to ensure more effective public participation in planning.

It is difficult to believe that workers employed by housing and planning authorities will have the independence to work with community groups in open conflict with those authorities on the issues that are the subject of the conflict. But it is perfectly possible for, say, a Housing Department community worker to help a rent-striking Tenants' Association to set up an old people's club and to retain a useful, if restricted, relationship with the Association on matters such as that. Some community workers would assert that such appointments, even on such a basis, would always tend towards the control of potentially subversive groups by the authorities. However, it seems to me that the variables are too many to permit easy generalisation about the long-term results of initiatives that are not explicitly controlling or subversive.

On the other side of the fence there are many community workers, usually employed by small voluntary agencies, helping community groups in working-class areas to fight the local authority and others on issues relating to urban development and management. And some community workers employed by local authority departments other than Housing and Planning (such as Education and Social Services) have also done this. Among the voluntary agencies Student Community Action (SCA) is of particular interest. A large number of Students' Unions in universities and polytechnics now employ full-time Student Community Action organisers. Much of the work done by SCA groups within Students' Unions is of the traditional young volunteer type (play leadership, decorating, etc.). But many are involved in offering support, secretarial resources and academic expertise to groups in conflict with central and local government. At its best the level of competence and dedication is extremely high and the lack of constraints (apart from lack of resources) makes the SCA structure an admirable one for radical experiment.

With this four part classification (of community work related primarily to social work, education, community relations and urban management), as with the one proposed in the Gulbenkian Report, the boundary lines are not at all neatly drawn in practice. For example, a community worker employed by a Social Services Department might work with a number of clients' organisations, helping them, among other things, to secure access to resources controlled by the Local Education Authority, and such organisations might include one formed by black people concerned about the effects on them in particular of certain local redevelopment plans. It is the frequent irrelevance of professional and departmental boundaries to problems as those with the problems see them that has led to the appointment of a number of what might be called generic community workers. These are people who, even if they work for agencies with specialised functions, are not required to define their jobs in terms of such functions, but can set their own priorities in the light of those of the people with whom they work. An increasing number of these community workers have no other professional background, but have either trained on the job or taken one of a growing number of community work courses in universities and polytechnics. (Details on such courses are given in *Current Issues in Community Work*, Community Work Group, 1973.)

Mention of this last group raises the question of whether a community work profession, separate from social work and education, is developing. The answer is that this is half true. Something is certainly developing which is neither social work nor education as they have been understood in the past. But it is difficult to use the word 'profession', if only because many of those concerned find it objectionable.

There are a number of professional associations that community workers might join. Some, of course, are entitled to become full or associate members of the British Association of Social Workers (BASW) or of the Royal Town Planning Institute (RTPI). A pioneering body in the field, which mainly appealed to those working in social and community centres, was the Society of Neighbourhood Workers. The Youth Service Association changed its title a few years ago to the Community and Youth Service Association (CYSA). Community relations officers have their own association.

But the most important body from the point of view of generic community work is the Association of Community Workers in the United Kingdom (ACW), which was set up in 1968. The initial objective of ACW was to be recognised as a professional association for community workers. For a while it hoped to be accepted as one of the constituent organisations of BASW. But the other associations that eventually made up BASW refused to accept it as such. However, for a few years ACW continued to lay down stringent membership requirements and to concern itself largely with professional training.

The development of ACW in its early stages was strongly criticised in an article that appeared in the first issue of the *British Journal of Social Work* (Popplestone, 1971). The author saw the primary motivation behind this attempt to form a new profession in the fact that most community workers were semi-trained employees on the fringes of the more established professions who were banding together in their own interests. He did not see that this would necessarily benefit those with whom community workers worked. He also questioned whether any approach to community groups that did not have an explicit political theory behind it could be effective and indicated his personal preference for radical political theory and practice. While some of his specific comments were open to question, there is no doubt that much of his general argument was correct.

From late 1971 onwards there was increasing dissatisfaction within ACW itself with the notion that it could become a professional association.

Professionalism implies a client/professional relationship. The doctor, for example, acquires obligations to his patient as such. He is supposed to treat him to the best of his ability whatever he thinks of him as an individual. The community worker normally does not have clients in anything like that sense. Occasionally a community worker's help is requested by an established and cohesive organised group. More often the community worker goes into a situation cold or with only a limited number of contacts. It is meaningless to call the community the worker's client. He works with individuals and groups within the community (which may be characterised by radical internal divisions of interest and opinion). And his choice of groups with which he works depends, partly of course on opportunities, but also on the values and presuppositions he brings to the situation. (Because of this the term 'client' is avoided in this book. The term 'contact population' is normally used to describe all the people with whom the worker is concerned and this wider constituency needs to be distinguished from any 'core' or 'nuclear' group with which he establishes a particular relationship.)

Professionalism also implies an expertise that only some people have and a situation where people are only allowed to practise a skill if they have duly recognised qualifications. It is acceptable that only a qualified doctor may perform surgical operations. But if one were to say that only a qualified community worker could help to set up, say a tenants' organisation, one would have dispensed with that freedom of association that is vital to democracy. Moreover, many community workers see the central task of community work as the optimum reduction of the distinction between professionals and ordinary people over a wide area of activity, but particularly in planning and housing, so that the knowledge gained by professionals could be shared and not sold for salary. Anyone holding such a view is unlikely to favour securing professional status for himself. More and more community workers feel that, while there needs to be training to develop abilities, community work can not of its nature be defined as a profession with clear boundaries.

Criticism along these lines led to a liberalisation of the membership requirements of ACW at its annual general meeting in 1973, and the opening up of membership in effect to all those concerned with community work at the 1973 annual general meeting. This followed similar moves by the Community and Youth Service Association. It is significant that the two main associations concerned with community work 'de-professionalised' themselves in the same year that the British Association of Social Workers passed the 'professionalist' Motion 14, which called for a Register of professional social workers and the eventual restriction of social work posts to qualified workers, at its annual meeting in Blackpool. The Council, the governing body of ACW, now has workers involved in social work, adult education, youth work, planning and 'generic' community work. ACW has become more of a forum than a professional association and is increasingly concerning itself with the 'training' of community group leaders as well as that of paid workers. This radical reorientation of the community workers' own organisation took a mere five years.

The fourth phase and community work as a radical specific social movement

The 'de-professionalising' of ACW and CYSA might seem to indicate the opening of a fourth, explicitly radical, phase in the development of community work. There are, of course, those in a number of professions, including education, planning and social work, who would like to see a radical re-orientation of their own professional associations. But it is only in community work that there have been really strong moves in this direction.

Some community workers speak as though community work were developing into a politically radical, specific social movement. This seems to threaten us with a largely pointless ideological discussion about what community work really is. The term 'community action' is now in general use to indicate participation in or work with community groups in conflict with authority and it is probably better to use that term to refer to what does appear to be a new general social movement (Bryant, 1972). 'Community work' is a term which implies employment and it seems better to use it to refer to the activities of people who work with community groups for a living. And there are many, though they now appear to be in a minority, who work with such groups with explicitly conservative values or (more probably) who work only with types of activity that are more or less uncontroversial, such as play organisation.

Less radical versions of community work may continue to have significance if local authorities continue to appoint people to community work posts where the worker's range of activity is clearly defined and limited, or if there is an imposition of 'professionalism' in the forms of improved career structures and stricter training requirements from above. The authors of Current Issues in Community Work, who were mainly academics and senior administrators, appear to have envisaged developments along these lines and to have viewed them more favourably than most fieldworkers. This is particularly evident in their appeal to the Central Council for Education and Training in Social Work to play an increasing role in community work training in general as well as community work training specifically geared to social work.

The outcome of what has been termed here the 'fourth phase' of community work is, therefore, uncertain. It remains to be seen whether it will be a mere interruption in the development of a professional group or the beginning of a different kind of development.

Towards a definition of community work

Although the terms 'community work' and 'community worker' have been used freely in this chapter and the types of work to which they refer have been roughly indicated, no formal definition of the terms has so far been offered. This is primarily because at the present moment, since the terms are only a few years old and are being used by many people with slightly different meanings, a generally acceptable, precise definition is impossible. Nevertheless, the fact that an increasing number of people are being called 'community workers' and are using the label themselves suggests that there are common elements in their work which can be recognised. This in turn implies the possibility of and need for some formal definition of community work.

Perhaps one should say as a preliminary that the precise meaning of the word 'community' itself is not central here. There is a considerable sociological literature on that word. Much of the more recent work is concerned primarily to criticise ideological usage of it. Even so, most sociologists accept that the term can be usefully employed (Worsley *et al.*, 1970, pp. 246-59; Clark, 1973). But, apart from any technical sociological sense, the word 'community' is also used in a loose sense in many areas of social administration. This loose sense appears to have two connotations, both of which are present in the terms 'community care' and 'community home'. The first is that one is talking about a process that goes on outside 'institutions' in either the strict or the pejorative sense of the word. The second is that one is talking about an impulse to a better, more humane way of dealing with people (Johann, 1970).

Both these senses are present in the term 'community work'. First of all, there is the fact that much community work is concerned with political life outside the two great sets of institutions in government and industry. There is, secondly, the fact that most community workers are concerned in some sense with securing a different quality of social organisation rather than merely additional services. One common use of the word 'community' is, therefore, relevant to community work, although stricter definitions of 'community' may not be directly relevant.

The emphasis in any definition should be on the work done rather than on the word 'community' tagged on to it. A generally acceptable definition might run somewhat as follows:

'Community work is a type of activity practised by people who are employed to help others to identify problems and opportunities that they have and to come to realistic decisions to take collective action to meet those problems and opportunities in ways that they determine for themselves. The community worker also supports them in the process of putting any decisions that they make into effect in such ways as help them to develop their abilities and independence.'

Such a definition is fairly abstract. The nature of the help offered should become clearer in the chapters that follow.

A NOTE ON AGENCIES EMPLOYING COMMUNITY WORKERS

As a guide for the reader attempting to identify 'community workers' a list of agencies employing such people is given here. The list is not exhaustive and any precise categorisation is bound to be difficult. Moreover, most of the agencies employ other types of worker besides community workers. But the list may give the reader a clearer picture of the scope and limits of the field under discussion by relating it to agencies with which he has dealt or is familiar.

Clients' organisations

Under this heading are included all those neighbourhood organisations or federations of community groups that employ their own community workers. One of the largest of these is the *National Federation of Community Associations* whose officers provide a number of advice and support services for the individual affiliated associations.

On a more local level there is the *Association of London Housing Estates*. This is a federation of about a hundred tenants' clubs and associations on housing estates in London. The Association employs its own community workers and other experts whose services are available to individual associations, especially those just starting (Goetschius, 1969).

In addition to these two federations, a number of neighbourhood organisations employ people to carry out specific tasks for them, such as running adventure playgrounds or advice centres. (See, for example, Bond, 1972.) Such workers are often 'indigenous', that is to say, they come from the area in which they work and do not necessarily possess paper qualifications.

Community action projects and groups

Student Community Action has already been mentioned and for further details the reader can consult Barr (1972). In addition many university and polytechnic departments offer their expertise to local community groups who need such expertise to present effective cases to local and national government on such things as planning proposals.

A number of people up and down the country work for groups which are not, or are just barely, agencies in the normal sense of the word and which are working on specific projects concerning, for example, children's play or the organisation of residents in areas of multiple deprivation. An example is *Inroads* in Salford. Again on a more formal level, one fairly well-established community action agency is London's *City Poverty Committee.*

Community Relations Councils

The work of these bodies has already been briefly described on page 11.

Community service organisations

'Community service' has come to be accepted as the normal term for those forms of voluntary work in the social welfare field in which there is not a strong counselling element (Dickson and Dickson, 1967). This includes such tasks as decorating old people's flats, manual work in hospitals, play leadership, driving vehicles for social welfare agencies, etc. Most large cities have a youth community service organising agency. This may be within the local authority, as is *Youth Action* in Sheffield, or may be a voluntary agency such as the *Manchester Youth and Community Service.* These agencies are increasingly questioning the extent to which they should be merely recruiting labour for social welfare agencies as opposed to developing group skills and responsibility among the young people with whom they work.

Sponsored community service is now being used on a major scale as an alternative to sponsored walks by such organisations as *Outset.*

For those young people who are able to offer a greater part of their time the *Community Service Volunteers* organisation offers opportunities to work for several months at a time on projects for keep and pocket money. There is also the *Young Volunteer Force*, which has a relatively radical ideology and is increasingly employing full-time community work teams in various neighbourhood projects. *Community Industry* and new careers projects might also be seen in this context. A number of service-providing agencies rely to a considerable extent on voluntary help. One of these is *Community Transport*, an agency with branches in several parts of the country which offer transport and storage facilities on a non-profit-making basis to social work agencies and community groups (Easton, 1968).

Co-ordinating bodies

Inter-agency co-ordinating bodies are sometimes strong enough to be able to employ their own workers who, depending on the way they interpret their role, may be seen as community workers. The most common type of such an organisation is the local *Old People's Welfare Committee (Age Concern)*. Full-time secretaries of Age Concern committees will probably be involved in a wide range of community work, including supporting old people's clubs and working with groups of volunteers particularly concerned with the elderly.

Councils of Voluntary Service

Council of Voluntary Service was the name adopted by the majority of *Councils of Social Service* in 1974 after a period in which they had been confused by many with the new Social Services Departments. The name was selected in a poll of CSSs late in 1973 after some occasionally acrimonious internal debate about the relative merits of the names 'Voluntary Service' and 'Voluntary Action'.

Something of the past of the CSSs has been described in this chapter (p. 4) and, although it is very much an official history, Brasnett (1969) is a useful source of information.

Precisely because they have never emerged as the really strong co-ordinating bodies that some intended them to be, CSSs have tended (in the larger cities at any rate) to make a virtue of not having any very specific function and concentrate on setting up and then floating off new types of agency. These have included in the past the *Citizens' Advice Bureaux* (Brasnett, 1964; Brooke, 1972), which at national level are still associated with what is now the National Council for Voluntary Service, Old People's Welfare Committees and local community service agencies as well as casework and residential services. Today Councils of Voluntary Service tend to concentrate on four main areas of work.

The first is their original one of liaison between agencies and community groups, which they do mainly by collecting, processing and redistributing information and convening meetings on such matters as the Urban Aid Programme (Community Action, 1972).

A second (associated with the first) is in providing financial and administrative services for smaller registered charities (for which they take commission that provides an important source of income).

A third is in the field of organising volunteers. Many Councils of Voluntary Service have *Volunteer Bureaux* (Ferguson, 1974). These are clearing houses to which volunteers and agencies needing them come to be matched together. They may also be involved in projects that involve volunteers, such as literacy schemes. Or they may be involved with neighbourhood-based care activities by self-directed groups of volunteers.

The fourth and most recent sphere of activity for Councils of Voluntary Service has been that of working directly with neighbourhood groups.

Home Office Community Development Project

The Home Office CDP was launched in 1969. A central team in London has set up and supports and helps to monitor the work of a dozen CDPs in areas of multiple deprivation all over the country. Each CDP team consists of both fieldworkers and research workers. The teams have considerably greater financial resources than most community workers and (in theory at any rate) a close relationship with the relevant local authorities. The sometimes formalised dual responsibility of the teams to both the local residents and the local authorities has been a major source of difficulty and raised significant political issues (Bennington, 1972; W. L., Liverpool, 1973). The Project is an experiment with a time limit. It is hoped that it will be possible to judge whether it is worth while making this kind of heavy investment in the sort of areas in which the experiment is being conducted. Activities by CDP teams include establishing resident-controlled advice centres, play projects and adult education schemes and supporting groups demanding greater participation in the planning and administration of various local authority services. The teams have produced a good deal of mainly duplicated material about their progress. (See also Greve, 1973; Halsey, 1974.)

Housing authorities

The ways in which *Housing Departments, Housing Associations* and *Social Development Offices* of New Town Development Corporations are employing people to work with their tenants have been mentioned already (p. 9). See also Demers, 1962 and 1972.

Local Education Authorities

Local Education Authorities have been involved in community work for some time. One form of involvement has been the appointment of *Community Centre Wardens* to centres built by the LEAs. Much of the work done in the youth and adult education services of LEAs may also come under the heading of community work. In addition to this some LEAs have appointed *Community Development Officers* or (as they are known in some places) *Community Development Wardens*. Such workers have often had a very free hand and have even been able to work with parents' groups attempting to secure a greater say in policy-making about local schools.

Neighbourhood Projects

In a number of places *ad hoc* committees promoted by such bodies as the local authority, the churches and voluntary social work agencies have been set up to appoint community workers singly or in teams to work in areas identified as having major problems without the need to set up any particular structure or activity being written into their job descriptions. Examples include the *Notting Dale Community Project* (Mitton and Morrison, 1972) and the *Greenwich Project* in London and the *Moss Side/Longsight Community Project* in Manchester. In a sense the *Shelter Neighbourhood Action Project* in Liverpool might be regarded as a special instance of this type of group (Shelter, 1972). Sometimes the workers are resident in the areas in which they work. Sometimes they may be indigenous as are many of those employed in Liverpool's *Neighbourhood Projects Group*. Sometimes a single organisation sponsors such a project without insisting on having a good deal of oversight of it. An example of this is the *Friends Neighbourhood House* sponsored by the Quakers in Islington in London (Power, 1972). Again voluntary social work agencies have sometimes sponsored such projects while giving them a good deal of autonomy within the agency. Examples include the *Braunstone Project* set up by the Family Service Unit in Leicester (Twelvetrees, 1974) and the *Manor Project* set up in 1968 by the Sheffield Council of Social Service (Skipper, 1969).

Settlements

Something has already been said about the early history of the Settlements (p. 4; see also chapter 4 of Inglis, 1963). More recently the Settlements have branched out in a number of ways, including club work with the old and young, advice and information services, new careers, literacy schemes and the provision of resources for militant or minority groups (Riches, 1973).

Social Services Departments

Most readers will be sufficiently well acquainted with Social Services Departments for there to be little need for detail here. Most departments now have community workers, but their role and the extent to which all basic grade workers are expected to assume a community work role vary considerably from department to department. Some of these issues are taken up in the last chapter.

Voluntary youth service organisations

New developments in youth work which connect with community work have already been mentioned in connection with the youth services operated by Local Education Authorities. Much the same is true of youth work by voluntary agencies who are also experimenting in a variety of ways. One example of this is described in Smith *et al.* (1972).

2

Principles, values and objectives in community work

Introduction

As the comments made in the last chapter (p. 17) indicated, community work is not concerned with some special notion of 'community'. It is not helpful to talk of its objectives as being to promote 'community' or 'community spirit'. But the question of what the objective of community work is remains.

The Gulbenkian view

The Gulbenkian group said that community work was 'essentially concerned with affecting the course of social change through the two processes of analysing social situations and forming relationships with different groups to bring about some desirable change'. They saw this as implying three basic objectives. The first was that of involving people in decision-making. The second was that of giving people the 'personal fulfilment of belonging in a community'. The third was one of providing 'services for people rather than solving abstract problems'. All this is summed up on page 4 of the report in the claim that community work is 'part of a protest against apathy and complacency and against distant and anonymous authority'.

This was far better than much that had been said about objectives in earlier community work literature in this country, in particular that produced by the National Council of Social Service in the period immediately after the Second World War. The emphasis on change as positive and the implicit recognition that social solidarity is based to a large extent on the perception of shared interests both

24

represented advances in thinking. But this statement of objectives is still open to considerable criticism.

Much of the weakness in the Gulbenkian group's line of argument derives from the fact that they attempted to drag too many people into their new category of 'community work'. (This assertion is controversial and not all community workers would accept it.) Earlier in the report the group said that community work 'typically consists of work with groups of local people who have come into existence because they want to change something or to do something that concerns them'. This is fair enough and, as was said in chapter I, most of those who have been appointed with the title of 'community worker' are doing just that. But the report adds that community work 'also embraces attempts to relate the activities of social work agencies more closely to the needs of the people they serve. This may include inter-agency co-operation, study and planning, as well as similar action over wider geographical areas or aspects of social policy' (p. 3). By opening up the field in this way the writers of the report made precise employment of the term 'community work' difficult. Nor is this merely a matter of classification. Roughly speaking, the more eager one is to welcome those making decisions at a higher level on the community work bandwagon, the more optimistic one is likely to be about the possibilities of working with the higher levels of the establishment. This in turn will affect the behaviour one expects from a fieldworker operating with, say, a Tenants' Association.

The difficulty in the report's use of the term 'community work' becomes clear on examination of the more specific objectives it outlined (see p. 24). The first is vague. Whenever a decision is made those concerned are 'involved' in it, if only in unthinking obedience. Even at a high level of generalisation, the question remains: what power to whom? The second seems to hark back to older ideological uses of the word 'community'. One needs to be clear both about the sort of sentiment one is discussing and the social context in which it is activated. The third I find meaningless. It presumably has reference to the questionable use of such terms as 'public interest' in defence of policy decisions that are evidently not in the interests of less powerful groups in the public affected by them. Finally, the protest which is mentioned is a moralistic one, taking the form of denunciation of such ethical abstractions as apathy, complacency and distant and anonymous authority. If the report had singled out groups and institutions in our society they wished to see subject to attack or change in specific directions, their perspectives would have been clearer.

The lack of precision in the report does not only come from the fact that the group were trying to include too many people in the category of 'community worker'. It also comes from the fact that they were attempting to discover a consensus in a situation where this was near impossible. They were trying to describe social movements and changes in our society in ways that would be positive and appreciative and yet at the same time acceptable to those whose position is threatened by those movements and changes. They did this because they saw the future progress of community work in terms of its development as a profession. The professional model implies, among other things, a restricted code of ethics for the profession which all of its members and most people outside it find possible to accept. That this is difficult enough even in the field of medicine which is seeking to promote 'health', something universally accepted as good, is shown by the controversies over euthanasia, abortion and mental illness. Where the values under consideration are ones which are rejected by some or which mean different things to different people, as is the case with 'democracy', 'community', 'participation' and other words used in discussions about community work, then the elaboration of an agreed code of ethics becomes highly problematic. The attempt by the Gulbenkian group to find an ethical consensus for community workers was doomed from the start.

Controversies over values

The best that can be done is to face the fact that one is in an area of controversy and outline as clearly as possible the opposing opinions. This opens up the possibility of realistic conflict, which in turn opens up the possibility of alliances in many particular situations.

Community workers vary as much as social caseworkers in the extent to which they articulate the values under which they operate and the extent to which they identify with specific social and political movements in the process of articulating their values. Many of them will be eclectic, drawing their ideas from a number of sources and changing their emphases as experience in the field opens up new questions for them. It is possible to distinguish a number of clear viewpoints about what community work is 'for'.

But it should be emphasised that many workers will not fit neatly into these categories and will see their work in terms of two or three of the five objectives it is possible to distinguish in the abstract. These are 1. to promote economic development, 2. to activate consensus, 3. to assist the personal social services, 4. to educate people to deal with the complexities of modern citizenship, and 5. to encourage radical change in the established socio-political system.

1. The first of these objectives does not merit serious consideration here because it largely relates to the developing countries. In such countries ordinary people (in rural areas particularly) are encouraged by government officials and others employing community work methods to adopt new forms of agriculture or small-scale industry or to build schools, roads, bridges, etc. as part of the general economic development programme but in ways and in the light of priorities that the local people set for themselves. In urban areas of the western world (with which this book is concerned) this particular form of self-help hardly comes into the picture. The sort of economic resources to which we are accustomed requires far larger input than any normal neighbourhood could provide and involves specialist organisations covering wide geographical areas. There are initiatives to form co-operative workshops, food co-operatives and credit unions (on which see Skelton and Simpson, 1972). But these are intended to alleviate the social problems caused by unemployment or to secure a degree of economic power for one particular section of the working class. Such schemes are not insignificant. For example, in a General Improvement Area some two or three million pounds may be spent and much of this money will come from the area, which may be a poor one, and go to private contractors. A neighbourhood construction co-operative could be very important in such a situation. But the importance is in terms of well-being and relative power within the system, not in terms of overall economic development.

2. The second objective is that which was adopted by many in what I have called the second phase of community work which was particularly concerned with the promotion of Community Associations and similar structures. 'Consensus' is a word used by some community workers to describe what they call a method of community work, which they contrast with two other methods— 'campaign' and 'conflict'. But to say that the term 'consensus' merely describes a method is to ignore the fact that to use such

a method implies social assumptions, values and objectives. It seems preferable to speak of 'activating consensus' as a possible objective for community work and to say that this objective suggests the use of certain strategies. In the past a majority of community workers did regard their function as activating consensus (as do a sizeable minority now), though they would probably not have used the phrase. It is the objective that underlies much of the thinking in one of the principal British text books on community work (Goetschius, 1969). The view was that the community worker should help people to do together what they could do together because this would make life more pleasant all round. This meant that within a neighbourhood or wider area one would look for types of activity that were uncontroversial and help people to engage in them, and that one would help to reduce conflict between local people and the authorities by interpreting each to the other.

Behind such objectives lay two assumptions. The first was that by activating consensus in an area one would be helping to reduce internal tensions and thus creating a happier atmosphere. The second was that there was no real conflict of interest between ordinary people in a working-class neighbourhood and those who made the decisions in the Town Hall. Both assumptions are open to question.

There appears to be no necessary connection between activity in community groups and overall neighbourliness (Turowski, 1968). Social activities in such groups can be a means of evading existing internal conflict (Mills, 1965), or can, indeed, become the arena in which personality conflicts are acted out (Frankenberg, 1966).

Nor are all conflicts between local authorities and community groups due to mere 'failures in communication'.

The essential point is that conflicts of interest are of fundamental importance in all major areas of life in our society and, therefore, full consensus is only possible if people are prepared to restrict themselves to the trivial. Probably most people would agree that there is nothing wrong with promoting less commercial forms of recreation, which is what most 'consensus' oriented community workers have ended up doing. But, if that is what one is doing, one should say so rather than resort (as many such community workers have done) to ideological abuse of such terms as 'community' and 'professionalism'.

3. The third objective is the provision of back-up services to

the personal social services. Some have spoken of community work as having a similar relation to social work as that of public health to medicine. Chapter 16 of the Seebohm Report is one example of this sort of approach.

The meaning of this would, of course, need to be defined more clearly in terms of conceptions of the objectives of the personal social services. If one saw these services as being an eternally necessary, though constantly changing, part of society, then one would presumably emphasise the ways in which community work could give social caseworkers new resources. These would include providing volunteer help and enabling social workers to use group strengths to support actual or potential clients. If one saw social work as essentially a social movement working for change in terms of certain values, then one would emphasise the ways in which community work might help to break the 'cycle of deprivation' and this would bring one's objectives closer to the last two that will be mentioned.

4. A large number of community workers have a professional background in education, and for many community work is essentially an education process, sharing general aims with other forms of education. According to this viewpoint, 'community work' would describe ways of helping people to understand the complexities of modern organisation and the types of individual and collective action which are open to ordinary people. It would be an education in democracy. But the person who learns from the community worker learns basically, not by being taught in a classroom, but by doing and by discussion with others involved in the doing. And the community worker would expect to learn as well as to teach to a far greater extent than the teacher going through a course or syllabus.

A pure version of this objective might involve the belief that it does not matter very much how much the community group achieves. What does matter is how much is learned from the process, how far people engaged in a community project gain in self-confidence, in organisational and social skills and in their knowledge of society. But, naturally, such a pure view would be impossible to hold in practice. In order that people should learn from their experience, their experience must be good. People are more likely to gain in self-confidence and therefore more likely to be amenable to further forms of learning, if they meet with success rather than failure. Therefore all those who see community work

29

largely in educational terms must also think to some extent at least about its impact on politics in the most general sense of the word.

5. What has been said so far should make it clear that there is no necessary connection between radicalism and community work. Nevertheless, an increasing number of people are involved in community work because they see it as a necessary part of a process to bring about major change in our society.

It is a little facile to speak of this as the radical view of community work and its functions. The term 'radical' is a loose one (as it is used in this country) covering a wide range of political attitudes, and one should distinguish between them. In discussions about community work the adjective 'radical' is used by different people to refer to actions varying from legitimate pressure on a local authority department using the proper channels to the further extreme represented by the mythological burning down of the Town Hall. Similarly the term 'participation' is used to refer to processes along a spectrum ranging from improved public relations by the Planning Department to the community control of Free Derry or the Black Panthers (Arnstein, 1969). Different types of 'radicalism' involve different types of change and therefore different strategies for change.

There are radicals who have major reservations about the ways in which we are developing technologically and wish to introduce changes in some aspects of economic organisation. There are those who feel that western society creates problems for itself by excluding the majority from participation in decision-making processes and wish to establish a more 'active' society without necessarily introducing major changes in economic affairs or altering the fundamentally hierarchical structure of society (Etzioni, 1968). There are those who are simply for the little people against the big institutions. There are those who form part of the socialist movement who believe that the focal point for desirable change will be working-class control of the economy and stress the need for highly structured working-class organisations to achieve this. And there are those in the social anarchist tradition who might accept socialist points about the working class but be suspicious of some of the structures produced by the labour and socialist movements and lay greater stress on the spontaneous collective action of ordinary people.

All these different viewpoints and their variants would lead to differences in at least emphasis in community work practice by those who held them. The populist is likely to find himself in a constant shifting of focus as groups of 'have nots' become groups of new 'haves' (Alinsky, 1969). The socialist, whether in the social democratic or bolshevik tradition, who believes in the central importance of the party, is under a constant temptation to use clients' organisations or community groups as mere sources of recruits for the party. At any rate he is less likely to find it possible to adapt to the pace of many social movements than a member of such libertarian organisations as Solidarity or the Organisation of Revolutionary Anarchists which stress the importance of the self-determination as well as of the organisation of the working class (Wooley, 1972).

As was said above, in practice most community workers adhere to objectives that represent some kind of synthesis of some of the objectives just outlined, most of them to a synthesis of the last three. They may see that their work is primarily, like that of social workers, with the poor and the deviant. But rather than envisaging this in professionalist terms, they may see themselves as contributing in a small way, though some community workers are inordinately ambitious (Cheetham and Hill, 1973), to a movement for radical social change. Thus they may see the process of educating people through collective action to more effective participation in civic affairs and other matters as being fundamentally subversive of our present system of representative democracy and leading to new ways of conducting government in which more people have more control over the circumstances of their own lives.

The political content of community work

Although only one set of objectives has been described in explicitly political terms, it should be clear that all the five objectives outlined have political connotations and that this is unavoidable.

It is possible to be a conservative community worker hoping either to restore an imaginary period of class harmony in a society of strictly prescribed geographical boundaries, or at least to promote primarily those types of activity that emphasise what people have in common rather than conflicting interests. It is possible to be a moderate reformist community worker, hoping to see some changes that will make the existing system of services more efficient and humane. It is possible to be a more radically reformist community worker, helping people to articulate demands which can only be met by major changes in the existing services. Or it is possible to be a revolutionary community worker, seeing one's work as part of the building of a movement that will fundamentally alter the nature of social relationships in a way that would be unacceptable to those who now hold power.

What is not possible is to do community work, to assist in the setting in motion of collective action, without affecting the political process and, therefore, without having political objectives that may only be implicit, that may cut across the established party political system, but which are there nevertheless.

Community work and the principle of self-determination

In this case it might be asked whether community work can be non-directive, whether it can respect the social work principles of self-determination and non-judgmentalism. This is sometimes expressed in questions about the right of the community worker to intervene in a situation to which he does not belong. This is a false way of putting the issue. One is and by existing one influences others. To ask whether one has the right to do so is at best a misleading way of conceptualising the problem. It probably derives from the use of the concept 'client' to avoid thinking through moral dilemmas in some other professional relationships. The principle of self-determination is open to philosophical questioning (Plant, 1969) and cannot reasonably be given the central place in social welfare values (Bernstein, 1960). The real question is not about the right of the worker to be there, but about what he is trying to do and on what grounds he justifies it.

The community worker, whose objective is in some sense to enable people to secure more control over their own situations, obviously cannot impose his own domination over a group with which he is working either by putting himself in a leadership position or by attempting to secure their half-comprehending adhesion to a point of view he himself holds. To do so would be to sacrifice the general objective to a particular one. Thus, while he may see his own action in a general political perspective which will imply lines of action he would hope the groups with which he was working would follow, his action must in some sense be non-directive.

This sense relates, not only to a general ethical principle, but also to a recognition of the facts of the community worker's situation. The first is that, unless one is going to resort to brain-washing or related methods of control, one cannot determine what the client of the caseworker or the contacts of the community worker will do. In practice they are free to reject the help of the worker, even if this is at some cost to themselves. (In theory one can debate at length what this freedom is.) The second fact is that we live in a period of moral pluralism and the existence of controversy over many issues means that the caseworker or community worker is likely to be uncertain of his own moral judgment, or, even if certain of it, unable to impose it in the knowledge that his action will be accepted by everyone as normal.

Speaking of self-determination in this more empirical way, it is easy to see why community workers need to be non-directive. The groups with which they work are often enough even less dependent on them than the clients of social caseworkers. Community workers rarely have any statutory powers. Because on the whole they take the initiative in making contact with those with whom they work, they have to make a greater effort to win acceptance, although this is less of a problem than is sometimes anticipated by newcomers to the field. And, if they are honest, most community workers will admit that we just do not know enough about the processes of social change to be able to say with full confidence what the long-term effects of any kind of community group activity will be, so that the priorities of contact groups can in most cases be cheerfully accepted (the main exceptions being when these involve action against even less powerful groups).

Honesty as a moral value

The principle that the community worker should be honest about his own values is closely related to the principle of self-determination and is insufficiently stressed in most discussions. It is a mistake to conceal one's own viewpoint on the grounds that by stating it one might impose it on the contacts. This underrates their ability to think for themselves and, as a line of action, is likely to incite suspicion about the motives of the worker.

It is even more immoral and shortsighted to attempt to secure an effect by giving a distorted impression of one's viewpoint. To take an example: if a residents' group expresses hostility to local gypsies, it is always a mistake to attempt to sidetrack this hostility by introducing a false distinction between 'real gypsies' and

33

'tinkers'. This is a tactic that has been tried by some local councillors with guilt-stricken liberal consciences when under attack on this issue by their electorates. The confusion which is introduced into the issue will only stave off active hostility for a while and may make it worse in the end by increasing the frustration of the local people who feel that no-one takes them seriously. A straightforward defence of minority groups (as long as this is accompanied by suggestions for positive action and is not merely a way of satisfying the worker's own conscience) is more likely to win the respect of the local people and even lead them to reconsider the situation.

Conclusion

Like the last chapter on the identity of community work, this chapter on values and objectives may appear a fuzzy account of a confused situation. Some would see this confusion or conflict over values coming to an end with the universal acceptance by community workers of some fairly precise set of principles. Others would see the situation as being fundamental to community work. Community workers are not necessarily more radical than social caseworkers. They do tend to be more articulate about the political pre-suppositions that underlie their work than many caseworkers (Epstein, 1970). This is one reason why large conferences on community work have such difficulty in getting off the ground. They tend constantly to return to a debate on basic political principles that might be discussed in many other settings and are barely related to the day-to-day tasks of community workers.

There are some moves at present to make participation (rather than improvement in services or the promotion of community sentiment) the central objective of community work and, therefore, the starting point for the elucidation of principles. This is in part a reaction against the increasing centralisation of power involved in the expansion of the Common Market, the creation of the 'super-ministries', the re-organisation of local government, increasing monopoly in industry, and the failure to develop the moves towards greater participation made in the 1968 Town and Country Planning Act. Participation as an objective is open to criticism on the grounds that it impedes efficiency, although there are answers to that (Bodington, 1973). A more basic objection is that, as was said earlier in relation to the similar concept of 'radicalism', the term 'participation' can mean too many things. The concept is intimately linked with classic democratic theory (Pateman, 1970). But any contemporary use of classic theory to define participation or what community work pre-supposes (Currams, 1971) must take into account the discoveries of social science in the last two hundred years. This point leads into the discussion that follows in the next chapter.

3

Analysis and the selection of objectives

The contribution of general theoretical perspectives

In any activity concerning human relationships general theoretical perspectives provide an essential mediating point between moral values and empirical situations. The study of broad approaches to sociology could, therefore, make an important contribution to the understanding that community workers have of their role.

'Formal sociology', the study of recurring patterns of group structure with the focus on the forms of those structures rather than their content in terms of meaning and values, has a good deal to offer community workers. In particular, Simmel's stress on the role of conflict in determining the development of group structures provides a useful antidote to moralistic approaches to the question of social solidarity (Simmel, 1971). It is regrettable that, whereas there are formal studies of small groups and of large organisations, there are few such studies of small organisations of the type with which community workers are often concerned.

But enthusiasm for the contribution of 'formal sociology' has to be moderate. There is evidence to suggest that patterns of group structure and relationships that appear in 'laboratory' groupings do not necessarily appear in long-term, natural groups. The focus on form rather than content rests in the end on a philosophical distinction which is at least open to question and this focus has theoretical weaknesses that are particularly important to community work. For example, formal sociologists have rightly pointed to a distinction between realistic and unrealistic conflict. But their approach to the matter does not in itself offer a firm basis for deciding when a conflict is realistic (Coser, 1954; Deutsch, 1969). Social science is inevitably concerned with content or meaning as well as with form.

One approach to meaning that has been influential in sociology in the Anglo-Saxon countries is that generally known as 'structural functionalism'. There are many varieties of this approach, but all lay emphasis on the ways in which different aspects of a society relate to and mutually support each other, giving it a degree of coherence of form and meaning (Demerath and Peterson, 1967; Isajiw, 1968). If structural functionalism were defined merely in such terms, then it would not be stretching its meaning too far to call Karl Marx a structural functionalist. However, there has been a tendency among structural functionalists to lay emphasis on both the relative equality of significance of different aspects of social organisation and on the degree of consensus within any one society. Marxism, on the other hand, suggests that economic structures have a critical role and that in our society economic developments are creating a situation with which society cannot cope without undergoing revolutionary change. It lays emphasis on conflict in society, which it sees in relation to a theoretical model in which all classes are related to two basic classes—the capitalists and the proletariat—which are in irremediable conflict with each other (Bottomore and Rubel, 1963; Feuer, 1959; Freedman, 1968).

The conflict between these two basic viewpoints is one that the community worker has to settle for himself before he can adopt a coherent attitude to his own society. An alternative approach appears to be provided by the extended use of 'exchange theory' (which has been developed in relation to small groups) in the analysis of society as a whole. This would see society in terms of exchanges or bargains, negotiations and conflicts between individuals and groups. It appears to take into equal account both consensus (the rules of the game) and conflict (the movement in the game). Exchange theory has recently been used to analyse the idea of participation (Godschalk, 1971) and some academics would like to see it given the sort of central role in community work training that psychoanalytic theory had in casework training at least until recently. This is objectionable because exchange theory does not provide a solution to the issue. It evades it. The question of whether the emphasis should be on conflict or consensus remains. Just as social work courses are increasingly setting up explicit intellectual confrontations for their students between psychoanalytic and behaviourist approaches (in all their varying forms), so it seems that intellectual honesty requires that any community work course should set up a similar confrontation for its students between major approaches to sociology (both those already mentioned and others).

There are other theories and approaches in sociology which do not provide overall perspectives, but which make contributions to particular areas that are of special interest to community workers. The concept of 'social network' is valuable in the analysis of the constituencies of community groups (Frankenberg, 1966). Litwak's work on the relationship between formal neighbourhood structures and informal neighbourhood interaction (Fellin and Litwak, 1963; Litwak, 1960; Litwak and Szelenyi, 1969) is a useful corrective to moralistic approaches to the question, such as that of Bracey (1964). The stress on the meaning of urban spaces in the work of Chombart de Lauwe (1959/60) and of the Institut de Sociologie Urbaine in France (1968) provides a contrast to the more geographical approach to urban sociology in the Anglo-Saxon countries. Apart from its discussion of race relations, Rex and Moore (1967) offers an analysis of what the authors call 'housing classes' which opens up the prospect of a serious theoretical approach to the relationship between class and consumer position in a field particularly interesting to community workers.

But the values of the individual community worker, even when clarified by being seen in relation to a particular sociological perspective, cannot, of course, be simply put into operation. Their translation into more specific objectives will be determined largely by the job situation—by the nature of the agency in which he works and the nature of the contact population with which he works. It is with these issues that this chapter will be mainly concerned.

The nature of the agency and its effect on approaches to the work

The first aspect of the job situation (the nature of the agency) is important and it is a pity that discussion has tended to focus on some ideologically-loaded questions about the possibility of working within local authorities rather than on more specific questions about the administrative structures within which workers operate and the freedom of action and access to resources that they provide. A good deal of space has been wasted in discussion about community work for the local authority. It has been claimed, on the one hand, that only the worker from the voluntary agency will have the independence to work with groups in conflict with the Town Hall and, on the other hand, that only the worker in the statutory agency will have the position to influence directly those making decisions (Borley, 1972). Both sides in the controversy are over-simplifying. At least three distinctions have to be made.

One must distinguish first of all between those voluntary agencies that really are independent and those more established agencies that may be so dependent on the local authority and other sections of the establishment for money that their employees can have less freedom of action than those in the local authority itself.

Secondly, one must distinguish between workers in statutory departments who are working on problems that directly relate to the work of their colleagues and those that are not. For example, a community worker in a Planning Department might be able to influence decision-making more effectively than a worker from outside, but might find it less easy to work with groups contesting local plans than someone in, say, an Education Department. A related factor is the extent to which the community worker is fully integrated in the work of his department. For example, a Social Services Department employing a number of community workers could either attach them individually to casework teams or group them in a central team under their own leader. In the first case they would be under considerable pressure to work in close conjunction with the social caseworkers on such matters as community care. In the second they would have a good deal of support against pressure coming from other workers in the department. They would have more freedom of operation in setting patterns of work and would even be in a better position to deal with major attacks coming from within the authority on their methods of operation.

Third, one must distinguish between the objectives of the community worker, his colleagues and those in authority over him in the agency. The two naïve arguments about the supposed results of working in either a voluntary or a statutory agency cited above are really half-concealed arguments about objectives. Those in the debate who stress the advantages of working for statutory agencies are laying greater emphasis on the improvement of services through the use of community work as an alternative feedback mechanism to those already existing. Those who stress the advantages of working for voluntary agencies are laying greater emphasis on participatory activism and the achievement in the long term of a shift in socio-political power within society. The former emphasise consensus as a fact and as a value, the latter conflict as a fact and as something that is not necessarily evil. But, in fact, a conflict could arise in any agency, voluntary or statutory, between a community worker and others about the objectives and scope of his work.

It seems best, therefore, not to contrast voluntary and statutory agencies, but to look at administrative structures and the degree of freedom that each type of structure gives to the community worker in determining his own role.

One important administrative factor in the work situation of the community worker has already been mentioned. That is the extent to which he has his own support system or shares one with other kinds of worker in the agency. This is a problem which is already well known to social workers through debates about the optimum administrative structures for social workers in essentially non-social work organisations, such as prisons, schools and hospitals. Little time need be spent on the question here, therefore. A more problematic issue in some ways is the exent to which a community worker's function is defined for him.

An employing agency, by defining the function of its community workers, may impose constraints in a number of ways. It may, for example, lay down principles and values upon which the worker is expected to work and act. But, without doing that, it may also impose constraints by defining the area of his responsibility. It may define the geographical boundaries within which he must work. It may specify that he must work on certain problems or promote certain types of activity. It may impose on him functions other than those of pure community work, just as the local authority social worker is likely to be asked to do more than pure casework. Of course, while words such as 'constraints' and 'impose' are being used here, it may be that the worker welcomes such definitions of the scope of his work, as they give him a clearer idea of where he does have freedom of action and an argument on which to base demands for resources.

Using the variables which have been mentioned, it is possible to distinguish a number of types of community worker who are engaged in support of community groups.

1. There is the community worker who is assigned to a relatively small area which has been identified as having problems, but who is given no instructions on how he is to work or what sort of structures he is expected to promote. His initial task is to become

closely acquainted with the area and he may be expected to be resident in it. It is presumed that in this process ideas will emerge on local needs and possibilities for collective action and the role of the worker will be to encourage this directly and by giving advice, information and perhaps access to resources (such as clerical assistance) to enable these ideas coming from the residents to be put into action by them. It seems from the unreliable information available that only some 15-20 per cent of community workers operate on this sort of basis. Many of these appointments were first made in the late 1960s. For a while it was assumed that this general method of operation would enable residents to define needs for themselves more freely and that, therefore, it would be a pre-eminently non-directive method of working. There are now some who feel that, on the contrary, this method of working carries with it the danger that a strong dependency on the worker will be created that will impair the effectiveness of the project.

2. Some community workers who are attached to particular neighbourhoods or small rural areas have social centres from which they operate. These include some residential community workers, youth workers where they define their role fairly widely, community centre wardens, some arrivals officers on new estates and some settlement workers. The crucial factor is probably not so much whether the worker does or does not have a building, but what sort of responsibility he has for the building. Many community workers employed by Local Education Authorities have implicit or explicit responsibilities to maintain the fabric of their buildings in good repair and/or to see to it that the activities that take place in them are 'educational' as opposed to, say, bingo. Where a worker operates under these constraints he obviously cannot determine his priorities simply in terms of the needs of the residents as he and they see them. He will be forced more or less to work with the 'clubbable', with those who enjoy fairly well-structured pastimes. It is for this reason that many community workers have a blanket, and to that extent unjustified, suspicion of all workers who operate from social centres and why some workers operating from centres found it difficult to obtain full membership of the Association of Community Workers before the liberalisation of membership requirements in 1973.

3. Some community workers, even though engaged exclusively, or at least mainly, with small-scale community groups, do not operate within small areas, but have responsibilities for very wide

geographical areas. At the same time, like the first type of worker described, they have wide freedom of action to determine for themselves which sorts of activity they shall promote and support. Such appointments are becoming less common. They have had in the past a largely experimental function and were designed to test out the sort of work that might be done by community workers. As the commitment to community work has grown, so the need for this sort of appointment has diminished. For example, the post of community worker at the Manchester and Salford Council of Social Service was of this type when it was first created in 1969. But the new holder of the post who took over in 1972, after several other agencies in the two cities had created community work posts, was invited to select a particular neighbourhood in which to work.

4. However, there are quite a large number of community workers who operate over large geographical areas, but whose functions are more specialised. They are appointed specifically to encourage the growth and development of particular types of neighbourhood organisation or special interest groups, whether these are playgroups, tenants' associations, neighbourhood care schemes, advisory services, Community Associations or some other type of group. In such cases a good deal depends on how strictly both the worker and the agency interpret the brief to work with a particular type of community group. In the process of attempting to establish a particular activity in a certain area, the worker may discover other needs which either he or the local people consider of far greater importance than the need which would lead to the type of group he is supposed to promote. Groups of volunteers working on a neighbourhood basis are a good example of this. Workers in several cities have been appointed to promote self-directed neighbourhood care schemes (Cheeseman *et al.*, 1972). Their experience is that it is often easier to set up formal care schemes capable of dealing with referrals from social work agencies in some areas than it is in others (McGlone, 1974). But in those areas where there is resistance to establishing formal groups of volunteers there may be a good deal of neighbourhood help for the elderly and others in difficulty. One way of dealing with this which may be appropriate in particular situations would be to assist in the launching of a multi-functional neighbourhood group, one of whose several functions might be the running of a good neighbour scheme. It might be neither possible nor desirable for the worker in such a situation to restrict his contact with the

group to matters relating to its care function alone. A great deal, therefore, does depend on the willingness of the worker and the agency to accept the need for flexibility while retaining the commitment to specific types of action and concern.

5. All four types of worker mentioned so far have had work with community groups as their main responsibility. But there may also be workers for whom this is a subsidiary role. Someone, such as a general secretary of a Council of Voluntary Service, might see his main responsibility in the field of creating closer co-operation between agencies and organisations, but might also promote and support smaller scale community groups which appeared capable of meeting some unmet needs. Similarly a basic grade social worker in an agency whose main function was to provide a casework service might help to organise a community group to deal with a problem that was common to several of his clients and many who were not clients.

These are some of the situations directly related to agency structure and job description with which a worker has to come to terms in deciding how to plan his work. Essentially they concern the amount of time he has at his disposal for any one project and to a lesser extent they are concerned with the resources other than his own time and skills that he has to offer to the groups with which he deals. Obviously a worker who has been appointed to work for three years in one tenement block will have a rather different type of relationship with the people there and will evolve a rather different strategy from the worker whose task is to promote play-schemes and who goes to that tenement block as to a large number of other areas. Similarly, workers who have special responsibilities either for buildings or to promote particular activities will develop rather different relationships with people than those who are completely free to set their own priorities. And those who have resources at their disposal will again develop different strategies from those who can only offer people their advice, encouragement and experience.

Variations in the social significance of neighbourhood

Important as are the constraints deriving from the nature of the agency, they are probably less important in the end than the problems and possibilities offered by the populations with which the workers are asked to work. The social caseworker may have to interpret the functions of his agency fairly freely (or refer a case if he cannot) in order to meet the needs of his client and must diagnose the situation carefully to see how this should be done. In much the same way the community worker must analyse the area in which he is working to see what are the needs and opportunities for collective action (and, if necessary, refer on to another community worker or agency particular aspects of the situation with which they may be better placed to deal). One of the major skills of community workers lies in the ability to make this analysis of contact populations and deduce what sort of strategies have more chance of success.

Often the contact population will be selected on a geographical basis. The worker will take a neighbourhood or equivalent rural area as his basic working unit.

The first consideration must be the extent to which the neighbourhood forms a socially significant unit. Modern urban development tends to restrict increasingly the significance of the neighbourhood as a social unit, especially as the geographical centres for work and play become separate from the residential zones in the major conurbations. Some have felt that this was a bad trend which reformed town planning and community work intervention could help to reverse. Increasingly, it has been recognised that the trend has many positive elements and that social progress may be impeded if these are forgotten in the denunciation of many of the problems that have arisen in the process. (For one statement of this point of view see Cox, 1965.) While most community workers accept this, it remains true that most of them use the urban neighbourhood as their basic working unit rather than working on the level of local government units in the fields of inter-agency liaison, policy development or the promotion of special interest groups. There is clearly a need to specify why one should work on a neighbourhood level in terms of the expected significance of neighbourhoods.

We need to distinguish between different groups in the population. The locality does not have the same significance for all of them (Mann, 1965, pp. 155-65). A young child is very much tied to the neighbourhood, so that children and adults who look after them (especially when they do not have paid employment) form one natural focus for work done on a locality level. Adolescents who are beginning to establish their independence from their families are likely to be least attached to their neighbourhoods and to be attracted by peer-group activities that may take place some distance away from home. (This is one reason why attempts to develop facilities for young people within structures dominated by adults from their own neighbourhoods are often fraught with difficulty except in some rural and small-town situations where loyalty to the locality is still strong.) The adult who is married will be more tied to his locality and this is especially true of the housewife. But in most cases the locality will be the mere background scenery for the home. Only the housewife who does not go out to work is likely to make close relationships in the locality and the extent to which this is so will vary according to the characteristics of the area. In later middle age, when the children are more independent, a small minority of the 'clubbable' or the 'political' will again turn to voluntary organisations as a source of interest and satisfaction and these will often provide the leadership for neighbourhood groups. Finally, the leisure time provided by retirement brings a much larger number of people to an interest in small-group activities. The years since the war have seen a significant growth in the number of old people's clubs which have also increasingly shed the control or patronage of middle-aged organisers and have become more concerned with the welfare rights of the elderly.

All these comments pre-suppose the existence of the sort of family system in which the extended family is of far less significance than the nuclear family and in which there are still relatively clear distinctions of role between husband and wife and between generations. This situation is changing and is under ideological attack at the moment. Nevertheless, it is the sort of situation which one can normally expect to meet in this country and therefore it governs to a large extent the sort of response one can expect to invitations to participate in collective action on a neighbourhood level.

Apart from the fact that people of different age and sex are likely to be attached to their localities in different ways, one must also recognise the fact that the social significance of locality can be different for different types of community groups.

Any organisation must have some kind of geographical base, even if that base is the whole world. The criterion for membership of an organisation formed around a particular pastime may be interest in that hobby, but for convenience's sake the organisation may have branches in all major towns and cities. If the hobby is popular enough, there may even be groups operating on a neighbourhood level, either autonomously or as part of a larger community group. The anglers or chess players in a neighbourhood may get together purely because it is administratively more convenient to meet fellow enthusiasts from just down the road rather than from all over the world. The significance of locality in such situations may be very low, although interaction within a special interest group may increase attachment to the neighbourhood. This latter point is best illustrated in more rural or small-town areas where, for example, the local football club or brass band may be the battlefield for a continuing power struggle between different groups in a locality where local matters are strongly significant for most residents (Frankenberg, 1966, pp. 102-11).

Outside the purely recreational field the geographical base may be rather more significant in some circumstances. This is because a group may be concerned with political matters and many political battles can be settled to some extent at a local level. For example, single parents in an area may get together on a locality basis, not merely for administrative convenience, but also to bring pressure to bear on the local authority or local Social Security offices. But this is merely an example of community groups reflecting political and administrative structures and such a group would also be likely to be involved in a national campaign. The fact that the people are in a locality-based group may not make the locality as such of any greater significance to them. Outside their group they may relate more easily to people in similar situations in other areas rather than people in their own area.

To some extent the significance of the locality may be increased if the locality has distinct boundaries. Recently a large number of council estate Tenants' Associations were formed or re-vitalised in the process of a campaign against the Housing Finance Act (1972). It was a political issue and economic interests that brought people together. But council estates often have very clear boundaries because of their unity of architectural style. Therefore the process of forming local groups to fight a national political campaign may have been materially affected by the extent to which tenants were able to identify with particular estates. It is undeniable that council tenants' organisations and many other community groups are and should be an integral part of the labour movement (Bryant, 1974). But this does not mean that they do not derive a good deal of their strength from intra-locality relationships whether these already exist or are fostered in the process of forming an association. The limited, but real, significance of locality in the development of class consciousness needs to be emphasised as much as sentimental over-emphasis on the role of locality in class consciousness needs to be criticised (Westergaard, 1965, section 5).

The existence of distinct physical boundaries can, in fact, be important in selecting the contact population for a community work project, although one has to be sure that such boundaries are significant to the residents. Within limits it is probably more important to accept locality boundaries as the residents see them rather than to look for optimum size as those planning a service might do when defining catchment areas. Thus, if a fairly small area has two distinct sub-areas (say, an inter-war tenement block and some streets of terraced housing), it may be better to regard these as two distinct geographical bases. There are limits when one is attempting to build more comprehensive neighbourhood organisations. It seems from experience that, except in times of crisis, only some 2-4 per cent of the population in an area can be expected to provide any kind of active support for such a structure on a regular basis, so that too small an area cannot sustain a community organisation. On the other hand, too large an area imposes organisational strains. It would appear that for such neighbourhood organisations there is an optimum size of 1,000-4,000 dwellings. But this becomes less important when the group forms part of a mass movement (if only temporarily) or when the group is smaller, more specialist or more informal.

In many areas of our conurbations where there is still considerable population stability and where a good deal of employment and commercial recreation can still be found in the immediate locality, the neighbourhood may still have strong social significance for most residents. In the patterns of interaction that result there may be more room for informal than for formal structures and relationships. But important changes may be imposed on such a situation from outside, such as the arrival of large numbers of new residents, mass redundancy, large-scale redevelopment or even simple disasters (Miller, 1973). When this happens the very strengths of such an area may prove to have degenerated into a concealed rigidity which makes them weaknesses in the face of the new problem. If what has been gained in the past from a closely knit social network is to be retained, it may be necessary to create new and more formalised structures and such an area may benefit from the outside viewpoint of a community worker in appreciating the need to do this and acquiring the skills to do it.

To summarise: Not only are neighbourhoods more significant to some of their residents than to others, but the importance of the neighbourhoods to community groups can vary from one point on the scale at which the geographical base is a mere administrative convenience to another at which neighbourhood organisations become the stage for articulating strong sentiments about the localities and fellow-neighbours.

Variations in neighbourhood type

The outline which has been given has already indicated some of the types of area with which community workers may be concerned. One can examine this from another perspective by asking what are the important variables for analysing a neighbourhood.

There appear to be two such variables. The first is class, both in the strict sense of a grouping of people who have similar relationships to the means of production and may become aware of a common identity based on resulting similar interests and in the weaker sense of social status grouping. The second variable is population stability and the resulting acquaintance that people in a locality have with each other. Features of the physical environment which are the first to strike anyone entering an area are largely reflections and reinforcements of these two variables. That is to say, people in different social status groupings will live in different types of house according to the control their class situation gives them over their own situations in the housing market. This affects, not only the quality of the housing, but also the freedom of the householder to move or stay put. Therefore, the physical environment is not a radical factor. What is important is its social significance and, in particular, its significance for the people who live in a particular locality and may interpret its environment in ways different from middle-class outsiders, such as social workers and community workers.

Using these two variables of class and population stability, one can distinguish a number of broad categories of working and lower middle-class localities. In practice any given neighbourhood will have a number of individual features that need to be taken into account. But these categories provide a framework for analysis in much the same way that analytical approaches to personality provide a framework for assessing individual clients in casework.

1 The low-income stable area The first type of neighbourhood is that inhabited by people on low incomes who form relatively stable populations. Such areas, whether of old private houses or of inter-war cottage estates or tenement blocks built by the local authority, often provide the bulk of the caseloads of social work agencies. They are often stigmatised because of the fairly high levels of relatively harmless delinquency they have, or are credited with having, and what are seen as low levels of household management. This stigma is misleading in many ways and particularly in the ways it leads to negative evaluations of all the features of such an area. (On this point see the section on the Sheffield estate in Mitchell *et al.*, 1954.) Failure to sustain formal organisations may be wrongly ascribed to apathy and incompetence when, in fact, it reflects a suspicion of the promotion of any resident to a position of superiority ('getting above himself') because this endangers local solidarity which is egalitarian in basis. Of course, such suspicion may also reflect jealousy and rivalry. But one needs to discern which is in operation. Often attempts in such an area to establish, say, a neighbourhood care scheme will fail. Yet closer acquaintance with the area will show that a number of people are engaged in caring activities at a cost to themselves that would appal many middle-class volunteers. One does not need to put these initiatives on a proper footing. They are working and are, therefore, presumably on a proper footing already. The problem is to enable those involved in such activities to develop access to resources that they did not previously have. Similarly, one will often find that the very strong local networks that exist in such areas, among the women especially, can be used by the residents to conduct a vigorous campaign over a local issue. Again, the point is not to organise the campaign 'properly', but to help those involved to develop the strengths they already have rather than aspire to strengths they do not have. Another example is that a purely informal group of retired people or young mothers or teenagers may be able to use resources that the worker has at his disposal to make their socialising more enjoyable and enable them to serve others in the neighbourhood. In this sort of circumstance far more risk may have to be taken with resources than many local authorities would feel happy about, since formal accountability could be more problematic. The basic problem in working in such areas is to overcome the natural suspicion that will be felt against those 'in charge' (whether the community worker himself or local people with positions of responsibility in schemes) by recognising and working with strong local egalitarianism and closely knit social networks rather than trying to impose an irrelevant bureaucratic pattern of organisation. Another problem is to overcome the low expectations that people in such an area often have of their situation; expectations that reflect past failures. In such an area the blurring of the boundary lines between good casework and good community work should, perhaps, be greater than anywhere else.

2 *The zone of transition* One must be extremely careful in making generalisations about zones of transition, since a considerable mixture of social status groups tends to be a feature of such areas. Large residential areas were built fairly close to the centres of most of our large cities for the middle classes at various times during the last century. As family size and the servant population have declined, the houses in these areas have become too large for the social group for whom they were originally intended. They have become used increasingly for multiple occupation. This process was accelerated in Manchester, Liverpool, Sheffield and other cities where the presence of redbrick universities near such areas created in itself a demand for short-stay accommodation. Zones of transition have a mixed population. There are often many transients, including students. Then there are the very poor or those, particularly black people, against whom there is prejudice and who, therefore, find it difficult to secure more adequate housing elsewhere. Because of the occasional architectural interest and the proximity of the city centre, such an area often attracts young middle-class couples. And, finally, in pockets of smaller houses there may be older people who remember, perhaps with some affection, the time when they were living in a 'good' area with neighbours of higher social status than themselves.

Because of the presence of racial minorities and deviants, such areas often acquire a bad reputation among the respectable and a romantic reputation among the radical, neither of which is entirely supported by the hard facts when they can be unearthed. They include Notting Hill in London, the old Moss Side in Manchester and Havelock Square in Sheffield. They need more careful analysis than other areas precisely because the mix of the population will strongly affect the possibility and the style of collective action. On the one hand, the explosive mixture of black people, young middle-class intelligentsia and the very poor can provide the materials for movements which are radical in politics and lively in atmosphere, and ready to resort to forms of direct action which, with the best use of the resources such an area has available, can be highly effective. On the other hand, the sub-groups within a zone of transition may develop strong hostilities to each other, especially if it is in a city where racialist anti-immigrant groups have managed to establish a position of influence. Above all, as in the case of the first type of area, it is necessary to know the scene properly before proposing formal structures, as these structures may merely cream off a particular sub-group, probably the socially aspiring, and mystify the situation. Serious racial disturbances in the United States have frequently taken place in areas where there were apparently strong, specifically inter-racial community organisations. People in a zone of transition are likely to be brought together, not so much on the basis of a structure set up for that specific purpose, but by a recognition of diversity and, as far as possible, a focusing of aggression on the common enemies that people in the area may have.

3 *The long-established, middle-income area* One of the most difficult types of neighbourhood in which to work is the fairly long-established, middle-income residential area. There one is likely to find that there is little motivation for collective action and what formal organisations exist are specialist and strongly defensive of their own rights and resources. In such areas the retreat into the nuclear family household has often gone furthest and the best openings for collective action are probably among those most attached to their localities by age and sex. It is in such neighbourhoods, as well as more distinctly affluent ones, that the pre-school playgroup movement has, on the whole, flourished. One's strategy would probably be to concentrate on needs such as pre-school play in the hope that the experience of acting collectively would open up people's minds to other possibilities. It is, incidentally, in such areas that many basic grade social and community workers live. Implications can be drawn out by the reader.

4 *The new, middle-income residential area* It is often easier to work in more respectable council estates and owner-occupier areas in the first two years of their life. This may be surprising, as it might be expected that in some ways community work would be easier

where people already knew each other because they had lived together for a long time. Yet the absence of informal social relationships often creates a need and demand for formalised relationships. People who move to an entirely new estate may join together in neighbourhood organisations because this is one way of overcoming the problem of settling down, meeting people and deciding for themselves the nature of the neighbourhood to which they have come. There is interesting evidence on this from the United States where it is more normal for people in the status group under discussion to be geographically mobile, at least in earlier life, than is the case in Britain. This evidence suggests that in this group the more often a person changes house, the more likely he is to know his neighbours, not less (Fellin and Litwak, 1963). This is because frequent changes of neighbourhood have led people to develop skills and social customs that allow them to make superficial, but still useful and satisfying, relationships with new neighbours very quickly. In the early life of an estate there are also likely to be problems which result from the fact that construction is still in progress. Building faults become apparent and local authority and other services are not yet established. These problems create a level of shared aggression against the offending outsiders that helps to bring people together, As a result, it is often very easy on new council or private estates to establish relatively complex multi-functional neighbourhood organisations which will take up grievances, engage in recreational activities and undertake some form of neighbourhood voluntary work.

5   *The crisis area*   Sometimes a respectable residential area that has been established for some time is confronted by a major crisis. This crisis might be a proposed major rent increase on a council estate, a major planning proposal, policy proposals concerning local school or medical facilities or changes in local industry. When such a crisis does occur a situation frequently arises similar to that in the new residential area, that is to say, people are brought together in common hostility to the enemy outsider and build up a range of activities around the campaign which create new personal relationships. A complication is introduced into such a situation, of course, if there is already in existence an organisation (dating perhaps from the first days of the neighbourhood) which claims to represent the locality, but is too entrenched in a routine to meet the crisis easily.

6 *The area of the established and the outsiders* This final type of area is similar in some respects to the zone of transition. This is the area where an established population is joined by a new population of a different status group. One example might be the relatively low income working-class residential area which has a new owner-occupier estate built next to it. Another example might be the 1930s private estate that has a not very attractive municipal estate built near it. Or again, one might have an area which for various reasons was turning into a relatively good housing proposition for outsiders, such as young middle-class couples or black people or working-class families attracted from other parts of the country by employment prospects. In such a situation, even more than in the classic zone of transition, it is possible for organised conflict to develop between two distinct social groups. Any attempt to encourage collective action in such an area may precipitate such a conflict, especially as the needs of the two groups may be quite different. (For a description of such an area see Elias and Scotson, 1965.) Experience suggests that in such a situation it is inevitable that, if collective action develops at all, it will develop independently in the two groups. If the autonomy of each is recognised, then there may be security for both also to recognise the possibilities of alliance on certain issues or activities. The difficulty is likely to come if one side manages to develop strong formal organisation, but the other does not. Yet sometimes this difficulty must be faced head on. There is no point in hesitating to assist, say, travellers to take collective action to defend themselves against persecution simply because it is not possible at the time to win for them the sympathy of other local people.

Neighbourhood variation and organisational structure

The needs of the different sorts of areas that have been discussed may be very similar. In all cases people may need more resources, more control over those resources and more opportunities for discovering how they can help one another. What differs is the type of organisational structure that it is appropriate to suggest to the residents and the extent to which the worker needs to be in close regular contact with the local people. There are a number of types of activity which would probably serve a useful purpose in the majority of areas. These include political action on purely local decisions; political action on a local level on national issues, such as housing problems or welfare rights; recreation; mutual support and 'consciousness-raising' among particular groups; mutual aid and support for those in immediate difficulties; local information services through 'community newspapers' and advice centres; children's play; participation in the management of local services, such as schools; and action to impede the flow of capital from the neighbourhood. But the structural relationship between the collective activities that prove feasible will vary widely. In some areas, particularly in new and high prestige residential areas, it may be possible to establish fairly complex neighbourhood organisations which can bring all these activities under one umbrella in such a way that each has a good deal of autonomy but can benefit from the common resources. In other areas this sort of organisational complexity poses difficulties and it may be necessary to think more in terms of a network of smaller special interest groups which may themselves have little in the way of formal structure. Neither should be thought a substitute for the other. Each has its own special strengths and each is a response to a particular situation. What is necessary is that someone thinks out the problem of what structures are suitable at the beginning of a community group's life and throughout it. Issues raised under this heading are dealt with in greater detail in the next chapter.

Variables in contact populations for special interest groups

Similar considerations need to go into work with contact populations that are not locality based. These may be cultural groups, based on religious or ethnic identity. Or they may be groups with particular problems, such as groups of single parents. Or they may not be groups of individuals at all. The community worker may be trying to secure closer communication and co-operation between organised groups and agencies. In all these situations the worker needs to bear in mind the variables that will determine the success or failure of collective structures that may be established. These include the extent to which there is already some interaction within the contact population, the extent to which the population is stigmatised so that people may not want to identify themselves as being part of it and the extent to which there are shared belief systems within it. In general, community workers have not considered carefully enough the problems involved in setting up collective action where the locality is not the basic working unit.

The contact population and the rest of society

The community worker needs to consider the relationships, not only within his contact population, but also between that population and the rest of society. At one level this means seeing the contact population in the context of a general analysis of cultural patterns and the distribution of social, political and economic power—in other words, the issues raised at the beginning of this chapter. On another level it involves understanding various specific structures in local political life.

The community worker needs an understanding of all the major spheres of local government and other statutory structures, such as the Social Security system, together with the relevant law. This, of course, is similar to the requirement of a social worker. But there are some differences of emphasis. A community worker would need to know less about family law and more about planning and public health. He also needs to understand relationships within the particular local authority with which he deals. While there is a basic legal structure to all local government, there can be considerable differences between local authorities in the ways in which different departments co-operate with one another and in the use of permissive powers. An example of this is that some local authorities are far more ready than others to designate areas for general improvement, and that the degree of efficiency in inter-departmental co-ordination to deal with General Improvement Areas can vary even where there is enthusiasm for this form of urban renewal.

A community worker who does not understand the formal and informal relationships within his local authority will be less able to exploit situations that may be of advantage to the people with whom he is working. As long as the securing of concessions on specific issues remains a middle-term objective (and this is probably necessary if the interest of the local people is to be retained), then the community worker needs to help his contact group to gain allies and sympathisers within the local authority and not create a united front against themselves by merely rhetorical attacks on the 'bureaucrats and politicians in the Town Hall'. This does not mean that it is only by wheeling and dealing that one can hope to secure anything. In the long term success must come from the strength and not the respectability of a community group. But the building up of strength does require constant injections of success and only a fool will throw away opportunities to achieve this by gratuitous attacks on what in some circumstances will be the other side.

The community worker needs to consider, not only the local officials, but also the politicians. Councillors vary a good deal in the extent to which they are active in their own wards and in their attitudes to community groups. Many, of course, are suspicious of them and this includes many left-wing Labour councillors who regard them, with their demands for special provision for their own areas, as a threat to equal and universal provision of services. That these suspicions are not altogether unfounded is demonstrated by the Barnsbury affair (Ferris, 1972) and the fact that one of the few commercially published handbooks for community groups appears to be primarily concerned with defending the amenities of middle-class residential areas (Jay, 1972). Other councillors see community groups as an illegitimate challenge to the elected authorities and it is true that any case for community work or action must argue that there are deficiencies in the present system of local and national democracy and imply at least changes that would modify the present system in ways that many local councillors would consider unacceptable. Others will try to exploit community groups or else to establish positions of influence with them from which they can persuade them to support their party or at least be 'non-political'. Some will avoid contact with them in the hope that they will prove ephemeral, though few can afford to ignore even the most tin-pot local organisation that has an interest in local affairs for as long as only a small minority votes in local elections. Others again will support community groups while respecting their autonomy, regarding them as an important element in local democracy that can help the elected representatives to keep more closely in touch with local feeling. Some of these differences in response to community groups will reflect differences of political belief and of personality. Others will reflect the local political situation and whether a particular community group forms part of a relatively strong local movement or not. A good deal will also depend on whether the councillor concerned belongs to the dominant or opposition party on Council and on his own position within his own party. Circumstances such as these will also affect the kind of alliances that can be made between councillors and community groups. The councillors themselves operate under many constraints, not least of which is the sheer lack of time to do things. Less sophisticated community groups may fail to appreciate this and either discount all possibility of dealing with the politicians or else expect a friendly discussion with local councillors to lead to miracles and thereby let themselves in for later disillusionment.

The problems that any community group is set up to meet cannot be understood within a context that is restricted by the boundaries of the area itself. They will need to be examined in a context of local, if not national and international, politics over a period of time. One can take as an example the Housing Finance Act of 1972, a piece of legislation that was of particular concern to many community groups. This was not, as some Labour Party spokesmen implied at the time, an act of mere spite on the part of Mr Heath. The Act was a response to the near total breakdown in local authority housing finance that had been brought about by rising interest rates over the previous two decades and which had come to a head in the late 1960s. It was not, moreover, a totally new response. Many of the features in or implied by the Act were introduced by the Labour Party in central and local government in the late 1960s. These included rising rents offset by rebate schemes and a consequential encouragement to owner-occupation. The Act was to a large extent a tidying up of a series of decisions already made, starting with the withdrawal of the facilities of the Public Works Loans Board from local authorities for house-building in 1953. This being the case, any hostile response to the Act by tenants' organisations had to take the form of either a very widespread refusal to work the Act which was never feasible (if only because the determination to take such a step had been largely exhausted in the struggle against what were mainly Labour controlled local authorities in the late 1960s), or else the organisation of a campaign for a plausible alternative policy which would have forced the tenants' organisations to consider more carefully their relationship with the existing major political parties. Similar examples could be found in many other fields in which community groups are involved. The community worker will, therefore, need to understand the ways in which the groups with which he is working fit in with the local political scene so that he can help them to understand the situations they meet and engage in realistic dealings with the elected representatives.

It is not only the formal structures of local politics that the community worker needs to consider. Publicity forms part of the development of any local group and the worker must know what kind of influence the local media exert and when the publicity they offer is most likely to be favourable. He may also need to help them develop their own publicity beyond the level of mere leaflet-distributing in such forms as community newspapers (Beddington, 1972) and even community radio and television (Turner, 1973). An understanding of race relations, of the cultures of racial minorities and of the complex nature of the responses to them may be relevant in many urban areas. Industrial and business matters are also important. One may wish to seek the aid of the local trades union movement either because a community group considers itself part of the labour movement also fighting to secure working-class living standards or because a community group is engaged in conflict directly with an industrial or commercial enterprise because of pollution, redundancy or some other issue. Community groups may also have to deal with contractors engaged in redevelopment schemes for local authorities or with private property developers. In any of these instances a knowledge of how to obtain information about private business enterprises may be extremely helpful in a campaign. There is also the general background fact that different types of work situation affect the ways that people behave outside work, so that an understanding of the social situation in the dominant local industries will give clues about the behaviour patterns to expect from the local people when they are dealing with situations outside work.

Conclusion

There will, in fact, be many aspects to a local situation which will require of the community worker either a sound background academic knowledge or a good deal of experience and the ability to investigate and understand a particular locality in terms of local conditions, values and internal relationships. The requirements sound as frightening as those for social caseworkers and in many ways both are expected to have a wide range of knowledge. What this means in practice, for the community worker as for the case-worker, is that one has a sound and continually improving knowledge of certain issues that are constantly recurring, that one has the resources to keep up-to-date, particularly on the law relating to social policy, that one has the sensitivity and sense to realise when one is up against something one does not fully understand, and that one has the ability and means to find out what one wants to know from the experts. Community workers still badly lack many of the information resources that they need, though the build up of radical groups in such professions as law, planning and the media has tended to ease this problem, particularly for those working in university cities.

But, besides needing to understand the situation as he finds it, the community worker also needs to understand the development of community groups and the sort of interaction that goes on inside them. Otherwise he may be as much caught out as the participants often are by the ways in which community groups develop and as inclined as their members often are to respond to these developments in moralising and unhelpful ways. Some of the ways in which groups develop and in which the community worker can give useful support during critical phases of development are discussed in the next chapter.

4

The development of community groups and the community worker's role

Introduction

There are a number of areas of academic study which will help one to understand the development of community groups. A number of neighbourhood organisations have been described in published community studies (Centre for Urban Studies, 1964; Durant, 1939; Jennings, 1962; Mitchell *et al.*, 1954; Mogey, 1956; Morris and Mogey, 1965). The difficulty with using this evidence is that the groups have usually been of subordinate interest to the researchers and one has to look at a number of studies before patterns and their significance begin to emerge (Frankenberg, 1966). There are a few articles which focus on community groups (Mellor, 1951; Dennis, 1961; Brier and Dowse, 1966; Twelvetrees, 1971). There are some useful action/research reports (Festinger and Kelley, 1951; Spencer, 1964). There is a large sociological literature on social movements (Banks, 1972; McLaughlin, 1969). But, partly because they have not been important enough, the sort of social movements with which community workers are usually concerned are not often analysed. There is no commercially published study of the tenants' movement in this country, for example, although participants have published studies of Claimants' Unions (Jordan, 1973; see also Rose, 1973, and Frith, 1972), the Squatters (Bailey, 1972) and the pre-school playgroup movement (Crowe, 1973).

Studies in group dynamics are another field from which one can gain some useful guidelines for understanding the sort of groups with which community workers deal (Hare, 1962). Psychological studies of inter-personal behaviour (Argyle, 1967) and leadership

(Gibb, 1969) can also be instructive. On the whole behaviourist studies of groups have the same strengths and limits as formal sociology, while the focus of group studies designed to contribute to therapeutic group work is evidently different from that of the community worker, so that he needs to approach that literature critically.

Academic material on social movements and small groups can obviously be of considerable use in training for community work. But there is also a need for study by community workers themselves of the ways in which community groups develop and of the roles that they adopt in relation to those groups—a need to study the community development process (Biddle and Biddle, 1965). In the growth of community work method there is a need to focus on these matters as well as on the problems that provide the manifest functions for community groups.

The variety of community groups

Inevitably, given the scope of this book, what is said is still at a high level of generality. But, in order that some particular issues can be high-lighted, this chapter concentrates on one particular type of community group.

Groups, including the groups with which community workers operate, may vary in a number of ways (Gurvitch, 1950, pp. 269-348). Size is one important variable. Another is the degree of continuity, whether the group is one which will continue to meet for years, presumably with some changes of membership, or whether it is an *ad hoc* body that may meet only a few times. Groups may also vary in the degree of internal cohesion they enjoy. Some groups which ostensibly exist for a single purpose may have half-formed factions within them. Other groups (and this will be especially true for those workers concerned with inter-agency liaison) will explicitly consist of sub-groups which have met for joint action or negotiation over an area of difficulty or something between those two (like consultative committees with tenants' representatives in Housing Departments). All these variables will be related to the central one which is that of function, both manifest and latent.

The type of community group on which this chapter concentrates is the multi-functional neighbourhood organisation. This differs in many ways from smaller scale groups with special

functions (such as playgroups) or larger scale inter-agency structures. But it is a type that has elements that are also present at the
more extreme ends of the scale of size. This makes it a useful one
to which to direct attention, as long as it is kept in mind that
variables such as size, continuity, degree of internal cohesion and
purpose strongly affect the extent to which generalisations are
applicable to any one group.

The formation of community groups

The starting point for any group is the appreciation by people that
they have a shared need or opportunity or problem. Coming to this
is a very complicated process. Once a successful group (or on a
larger scale a social movement or a revolution) has started, then
it is easy enough to say in retrospect that, given the situation,
it was natural that people should have come together and acted in
the way they did. The fact is that most social movements have
taken people by surprise, including most of those who were in at
their beginning. This is true of the French Revolution and of the
success of the pre-school playgroup movement in the last few
years.

A frequent element in the situation appears to be disappointed
expectation. One can treat people pretty badly and they may be
cowed into submission, fatalistically accepting that that is all they
can expect. But, if people have found that their situation is
gradually improving in some respect over a long period and
then there is a set-back, they may well feel that they have been
unjustly treated and rebel. It is not the extent or intensity of
oppression that matters, but the fact that it runs contrary to the way
people have learned to assume that their world is run (Davies, 1962;
Gouldner, 1955; Runciman, 1966; Wertheim, 1974).

A number of things follow from this. One is that the initial
grievance leading to the realisation of the need for collective
action will often concern the failure of those with power or
authority to do something that they should on their own admission
be doing, rather than a demand for reform in the sense of a change
in the law or overt policy. Inadequacies in the repairs and
maintenance systems on local authority housing estates are a
common example of this. On the other hand, people may regard a
decision as unfair without appreciating that its reversal would
have much wider policy implications. Rent increases under the

Housing Finance Act are an example. Reactions in both cases may be similar, but in order to take effective action people will need to learn to distinguish between the two types of situation and organise their community group or campaign to fit the type of situation with which they are attempting to deal.

It also follows from the fact that collective activity often arises out of a feeling that people have been deprived of something that is their right that the move to collective action may be preceded by or involve a fairly radical shift in attitudes and this may lead to unrealistic appraisals of the situation. People of a relatively high social status who have grown accustomed to the idea that they have a certain limited power and who speak a similar language to those in authority may move fairly easily into collective action on specific issues without changing very much in their general outlook. This is true of many local amenity or conservation societies. On the other hand, a more subordinate group, conditioned to an apathetic fatalism relieved only by outbursts of anger or celebration, may respond much more drastically to the notion that their ill-treatment is illegitimate. Something very much like conversion may, therefore, precede collective action in some situations. During the 1967-8 rent strike in London, speakers at tenants' meetings urged their audiences to forget the shame they usually felt about debt and to boast of the fact that they were 'in debt' to the GLC because they were withholding their rent in protest. This sort of speech was often followed by people coming from the audience to 'testify', as one might have put it in another context, to the fact that they were on rent strike. The fervour generated in such a conversion process is an important source of strength. But it needs to be cultivated and employed and there is always the danger that it will lead to a false optimism about the strengths of the movement. Like any process involving a shift in self-image, the move to a new type of collective action has great creative possibilities, but also carries a degree of risk.

The community worker is often invited into a situation after a loose form of grouping has been formed by people who have begun to identify a need for action. On the other hand, many workers go into situations where there are known or presumed to be problems in order to stimulate collective activity around them. Those whose contact is made in this way have to begin themselves to bring people together to discuss common needs and opportunities. There are a number of ways of doing this.

1 Selling a model One can, for example, simply propose a course
of action to people and argue reasons for it. In some respects this
was the model of working adopted by those involved in what I have
called the second phase of community work. The fact that the Community Association movement had something of a blueprint for
community activity, specifically in the shape of the model Community Association constitution, meant that the role of the
community worker was often to sell the blueprint or model
wherever he could. Goetschius (1969) reports how community
workers from the London Council of Social Service decided not
to impose the 'balanced neighbourhood' ideal on small local
authority housing estates whose tenants regarded it as irrelevant to
their needs and special identity. And there is now considerable
suspicion of strategies that involve the selling of models. But a
community worker might still wish to sell a model for a number
of reasons. He might be involved with a broad but specific social
movement which wished to extend its boundaries still further in a
period of rapid growth. Many community workers co-operated with
local tenants' leaders in setting up new tenants' associations during
the passage of the Housing Finance Bill. Again, some workers have
a remit to establish particular types of local organisations, such
as neighbourhood care schemes or playgroups. And, if a worker
wished to help a special interest group to establish their own
organisation, he might well have to bring people together arti-
ficially in the first instance. This consideration would apply to
people working with PHAB (Physically Handicapped and Able
Bodied) Clubs, specialist claimants' groups, etc. Methods of selling
a model adopted by such workers might include distributing leaflets,
convening and speaking at public meetings, setting up well-
publicised bases in localities and appealing for help to those people,
such as clergymen and journalists, who have well-established means
of communication. But while there may still be reasons for wanting
to sell a model today, most community workers would still in
such circumstances retain a greater degree of flexibility than was
normal up until the 1950s and recognise more openly the need to
adopt whatever model is being used to particular circumstances.

2 Ultra non-directive methods The third phase of community
work involved, among other things, a reaction against the strategy
of model-selling and, as was said in the first chapter, this led to the

development of what were sometimes extremely non-directive methods of working. A central notion here was that there were considerable advantages in a worker or team being based in one locality for a fairly lengthy period of time, perhaps several years. The initial stages of such a neighbourhood project would involve spending three to six months 'hanging around' in as purposeful a way as possible. Conversations would be struck up in places where this was conventionally acceptable, such as launderettes, shops, bus queues and children's play areas. Gradually the worker would become part of the local informal networks and would begin to learn what people in the locality saw as their problems. The worker could then use both the networks and the information to begin to bring people together to discuss common needs in a way that would still leave the greater initiative with them. Examples of this approach are given in the section on neighbourhood projects in the 'Note on agencies employing community workers', though not all the agencies named there adopted this approach to its full extent.

The approach has a number of advantages, especially for more settled areas which are likely to be suspicious of ideas introduced by outsiders and quietly sabotage them even while appearing to show interest. It also has many drawbacks. It is, for one thing, uneconomic in terms of the worker's time and salary. There is no evidence that the ideas for collective action that come out of such processes are much different from those proposed by workers who go into situations and begin to canvass support for them immediately after they have analysed the areas for themselves. Local interpretations of local needs are not necessarily correct. For example, a group may give themselves an official title that includes the name of the locality in which they live and thereby make some claim to speak for the whole area. In fact, they may speak for the (perfectly legitimate) interests of one part of that area only and the rest may be hostile to their views, although less vocal. A common instance of this is in areas proposed for clearance where a pocket of owner-occupiers may claim to speak for the whole area, not only for themselves, whereas the tenants in the rest of the area may be in favour of clearance as a quick route to a council house and against the group's proposal to turn the area into a General Improvement Area. If this separation of interests is recognised from the start, then a compromise solution may be possible. But, once a group has made an invalid claim to speak for a whole area, it is difficult to withdraw this claim without losing face, so that after a while a compromise solution becomes impossible. In such a situation a worker who simply respected the group's right to interpret its own role would be doing it a disservice. A final disadvantage of extremely non-directive approaches to community work is that because the worker is drawn into the local social networks, there is a strong possibility that a dependency situation will be created in which all community projects rely on the worker's presence. The one extensive report on a project conducted on a highly non-directive basis indicates as much (Mitton and Morrison, 1972).

3 *Direct non-directive approaches* Many community workers, either on principle or because of circumstance, operate in ways that look like compromises between the directive model-selling approach and the ultra non-directive approach. One such method is to conduct a survey in an area which asks about the area's problems and the action respondents feel would be appropriate. One advantage of using a questionnaire survey is that at the initial point of contact it gives the worker what is becoming a universally recognised and largely accepted role. For some reason people will talk to someone on their doorstep who says he is doing a survey when they might be much more reluctant to get into conversation without this explanation of his presence. At the end of a brief survey one should have a clearer notion of what local feeling is on various issues, have started people thinking and have a list of individuals who have expressed interest in being actively involved. These can then become a core group in which matters can be discussed further before, if that is necessary, a second and more direct approach is made to the contact population as a whole. (Of course, as such a survey is directed to a form of recruiting rather than to the gathering of knowledge, it need not be subject to the same criteria as a sociologically respectable survey would be, and its findings cannot be used as though it were such a survey.)

4 *Use of relatively extensive resources* All the ways into a situation that have been described so far have involved the use mainly of the worker's time. It may be that some workers will have other resources at their disposal and can use these to initiate change and moves to collective action. By employing money or other resources in consultation with local people to establish new services he may be able to create new senses of what is possible and help people to initiate further local activity. This is one way of

getting fairly quick results, but the disadvantage is that experience suggests that it is difficult sometimes to persuade local people to take over responsibility for a service established by a professional worker even when the money to meet the costs is available.

5 *Use of a role other than that of community worker* Some professional workers whose main task is not community work may use their major function as a basis for making contact with local people and leading them into collective activity. Such people might include social workers, youth club leaders, adventure playground organisers and headmasters of community schools. Indeed, someone might set up, for example, a welfare rights advisory service in a neighbourhood less for its own sake than to establish a position in the area. Such an approach has the advantage of giving the worker a ready-made explanation of his presence in terms that are more immediately comprehensible and thus help him in the initial period of a project. On the other hand, there may well be a tension between the community worker role and the other role, and experience suggests that it is difficult to work from a position of dealing with individual clients to one in which those clients are brought together in collective action.

The establishment of group structures

Once a group has got together in some way and begun to identify a need, the next stage is to move towards establishing a structure. Here the community worker may have an important role in relaying the experience of groups tackling similar issues and in helping the group to identify more precise objectives in the light of his knowledge of relevant areas of social policy and administration.

The formal structure that is developed needs to be related to two matters—the manner in which the group came together and the precise function it is going to assume.

The second matter is probably the more important. But the first should also be taken into consideration. If a group has formed on the basis of local informal networks, then the structure should be built around these and not ignore them. If the group has formed as part of a rapidly growing social movement and in an atmosphere of great enthusiasm, it may be necessary to take more people into the committee than would be appropriate in a more routinised organisation and to make greater use of general meetings. If the group has started in a new residential area or has been started by bringing people with special interests together from over a wide area, then a fairly well-defined structure may be preferable, unless the constituency is such that it is likely to be put off by formality. What is necessary is to avoid dogmatic preferences for either well-defined, complex structures or for more informal structures under greater popular control. Effective democracy requires different structures in different settings.

But function is necessarily the most important determinant of structure. A small specialised group, such as a playgroup or an old people's social club, may need very little in the way of formal organisation. A neighbourhood care scheme, whose main concern is to be efficient in its task, will probably need no formally democratic structures and procedures at all. An association with pretensions to speak for all the people in an area will need a well-defined system of popular control, if only to secure credibility. A campaign organisation will need to be structured in such a way as to involve as many people as possible, but at the same time will need a very effective centre able to make quick decisions in response to events. On the other hand, one might have a long-standing neighbourhood organisation with many functions that were given over to more or less autonomous sections in some kind of liaison with a central committee which undertook common tasks. Where large sums of money are involved there is an evident need for a system to maintain checks on spending. Similarly, where professionals are concerned with basically working-class community groups or clients' organisations, the structures need to be designed in such a way that control rests and is seen to rest with the people for whom the organisations exist.

Some of these points about structure may be made clearer by detailing possible varieties of structure for groups of the same type.

For example, a neighbourhood care scheme might be:

A natural extension of the activities of an informally organised social centre in a fairly stable area.

A small, tightly organised group of volunteers with high morale, frequent group meetings making for improved possibilities of training of some kind, and high reliability in dealing with referrals from professional agencies.

A larger organisation with a more authoritarian structure in which leaders passed referrals on from agencies to volunteers and in which, again, there was high reliability in dealing with referrals.

A section of a larger neighbourhood organisation able to call on the resources of the larger body on special occasions.

A federal body linking a number of pre-existing school, church and other volunteer groups which built on, co-ordinated and extended initiatives to which people already felt committed and could assist professional agencies in finding appropriate volunteers.

Similarly, a council estate tenants' organisation might be:

An organisation set up mainly to campaign over a particular issue run on a basis of frequent and regular decision-making public meetings with active roles (e.g. street organiser) given to a large number of members and a strong leadership core with charismatic features.

An even more informal body based on a small area grouped around one or two individuals recognised as being competent by local people to speak for them.

A highly routinised body with a strong federal structure in which there were a number of semi-autonomous sections for which the central committee acted as a co-ordinating mechanism.

A body with a similarly wide range of activities but with a stronger central committee and weaker autonomy for sections making it easier to deploy all the resources of the organisation on a temporary (not necessarily political) campaign.

The observations that have been made about structures are matters of common sense which a community worker can put to people hoping to form an organisation if necessary. The difficulty is that in deciding structures people often bring models from other situations which are inappropriate.

Many people who become involved in working-class community groups have experience in the trade union movement and perhaps in labour politics. They may bring to the formation of a new type of working-class organisation unarticulated assumptions about the need for structural discipline which are derived from their experience and which do not fit the new situation. Since the work situation as we have it imposes a considerable discipline on workers and since the trade unions face an organised, strong and relatively centralised other side, the labour movement has developed organisational models which have strong centralist elements and which rely for their successful working on the fact that collective action, once set in motion, is relatively easy to maintain in an industrial situation. Creating structures for working-class community groups on these lines may lead to a lack of attention to the real strengths of such groups, for example the social control imposed by housewives' gossip, and thus be quite inappropriate. Of course, many people with experience in the labour movement are quite able to see this for themselves. But, where community group leaders with such experience do not see it, enormous problems can result. Too often in the past the council tenants' movement has concentrated on building up imposing administrative structures in the name of the 'unity of tenants' while giving too little attention to the problems of mobilising the base. One extreme example of the inappropriate use of trade union experience was provided during a rent strike in a northern city by a Tenants' Association leader who was a trade union official and who not only did not use the potential support he had from local housewives, but expressed displeasure that 'females' were showing a greater interest in the rent issue than men. 'The way I look at it,' he explained, 'a rent increase is a wage decrease. It's men's business, not females'.' This was in a city where the successful Tenants' Associations were precisely those in which women held key leadership positions.

At the other extreme, in several community groups models are introduced by middle-class radicals which under-estimate the potential value of formal structures in encouraging group purpose and solidarity. Used to the unspoken discipline of group discussion, these people are sometimes unaware of the fact that they are able to cope with certain types of group interaction to which others may be unaccustomed. When they succeed in forestalling attempts to establish formal structures they begin, by their sheer skill in group situations and without conscious manipulative intent, to create covert structures in which they have effective leadership because their less skilled fellow members are lost in what appears to be a shapeless situation (Freeman, 1973). This is one of the reasons why clients' organisations sometimes get controlled by cliques of middle-class drop-outs who belong to the client category concerned but are untypical of the mass of those in it. At worst this development can lead to the death of the group.

A third model which is often used inappropriately is that of the discrete pressure group. Those who have experience in working with such groups as Civic Societies and professional associations which have succeeded in persuading local government officials and others to adopt changes in policy often attempt to impose strategies and structures which are based on that experience in cases where the issues are more fundamental or controversial. Thus they may establish structures that do not sufficiently involve the base in a campaign because their experience does not suggest that they do so. And this may lead them to failure.

If a group is in danger of establishing itself with a formal structure that is inappropriate, it is obviously part of the community worker's role to put some of the issues involved to people so that they can make more realistic decisions. What this means in practice may be very complicated. The decisions will probably be made in part at public meetings in which subtleties do not come across very easily. It may be counter-productive to react in a simply critical manner to one suggestion, even if it comes from another person only half-inside the contact population, such as a local councillor, clergyman or social worker. How far the worker does have an opportunity to help people really to discuss the issues involved in forming structures will depend on such things as his own reputation in the area, how well the meeting has been prepared, whether there are people with strong ideological motivations at the meeting, how large and cohesive the meeting is, and so forth. One significant point to remember is that formal structures are often altered quite radically in practice. It may be easier to talk issues through in the day-to-day work of a new group than in what may be an emotionally and ideologically-loaded debate about a written constitution. It sometimes happens that when a group has been setting itself up as a formally constituted association one faction has insisted on innumerable constitutional safeguards and, once assured by the inclusion of these, has assisted in the development of much more informal procedures in the months that followed.

Later crisis stages in the group's development

The move from the identification of needs to the formation of an actual group structure is an awkward one. People may feel strongly that 'something ought to be done about it' and gain consolation, or even inspiration, from their agreement on that point. When they move from there to the creation of an organisation they put themselves at risk in several ways. They are testing the truth of their previous assertions. They risk being public failures. They may be coming into conflict with powers and authorities of whom they are afraid. At the very least they are probably letting themselves in for a good deal of work for uncertain rewards. There is likely, therefore, to be an intervening stage of doubt and uncertainty. This is one reason why they should not normally be encouraged to allow too much time to elapse between the formation of the original core group and the move to set up an organisation proper.

But once the formal organisation is established there is likely to be an initial spurt of enthusiasm. The very fact that the group has been set up will give a sense of achievement and this may be matched by actual achievements. There will be a great deal to do in the early days when things are not routinised and there will probably be an increasing degree of interaction between the leaders in particular and to a lesser extent between all members. It is also likely that some kind of group identity will be created which may be reinforced by a spoken or unspoken group ideology.

For all these reasons the atmosphere inside the core group (the committee in a relatively large formal organisation, the frequent attenders in a smaller, informal group) will probably be optimistic and self-confident at first and people will derive a good deal of satisfaction from their participation in it.

At this stage the community worker's main role (if there is a need for an outside worker at all) is likely to be in the form of giving advice and information. The group may want information on the law relating to charity status and to gaming (if they are concentrating on recreation) or on the possibilities of obtaining grant aid. They may need information about the law relating to housing, planning or public health, if they are in conflict with the local authority over an issue relating to urban development. They may also need advice on ways of conducting a campaign or on elements of a campaign, such as organising a demonstration or seeking publicity in the local press. Sometimes the community worker may be asked to act as a mediator between a group and the local authority, where negotiations are feasible. The worker may also be able to obtain various resources for the group, such as specialist professional advice or money or buildings or clerical help. But, both in giving information and in making resources available, the worker should always be careful not to give where it is not necessary, in order to avoid dependency. If large resources are required (such as a community centre building), it is better, when possible, to hand over complete control to the local people. This is so even though they may test out their powers over these resources in fairly destructive ways for an experimental period or simply fail to come to grips with all the administrative problems involved.

While the worker is playing this role he also needs to watch what is happening in the organisation, because this honeymoon situation conceals and even helps to develop situations which may prove hampering to the community group at a later period. He needs to look at whether internal conflicts are developing within the core group. These may be mere personality conflicts or they may be conflicts over aims or ways of approaching problems. The increasing solidarity within a core group may be at the expense of its contact with the base it claims to represent or help. It becomes, in short, a clique. In some cases, individuals in the core group may discover that they have talents they had not appreciated before and may begin to mix socially with people from new backgrounds (such as the community worker himself) and this may lead them to adopt new reference points which isolate them from other members of the group. In an extreme situation the leaders may begin to develop scapegoating of the ordinary members—what one community work team called the 'martyrdom complex'—as a means of evading the problems of the organisation (Spencer, 1964).

Any developments of this sort will probably emerge in the next phase, that in which the group comes to terms with the issues that first brought it into existence. This is likely to happen anywhere between three months and two years after the formation of a community group.

If the group was originally brought together to bring pressure to bear on an authority, then sooner or later it will be clear that, for the time being at least, the battle has been won and lost. The community group may have gained its point or it may no longer be able to secure enough support to bring effective pressure to bear or there may have been some concession by the authority. At this stage the group might quite rightly decide to cease existence. This could happen with certain types of campaign, for example against specific local planning proposals. On the other hand, the group may have been set up for the sake of an activity of a relatively simple kind and can, after the initial spurt of enthusiasm, settle down to a routine. Another situation again is that of the community group which has a complex of activities and finds that after the initial phase of hectic activity it needs to re-examine its priorities. This may be because the group intended from the start to be a multi-functional organisation and is simply considering its early experience. On the other hand, it may be that the group formed in order to make a protest and in the course of making that protest has established recreational and welfare activities for the sake of raising money and morale and that these activities now seem valuable in themselves. A complex of activities can provide an organisational base for future protests of a major kind or the continual raising of minor issues, none of which on its own would merit the formation of an organised group. In either of these cases— that in which the various functions were intended from the start and that in which other functions have been created in the course of a protest campaign—the ending of the first phase poses potentially severe problems for the group. The very fact that it has a multiplicity of functions means that it has within it a number of special interests and viewpoints which are in potential conflict. The debate over the re-assessment of priorities may bring these into the open. Where a distinct shift in priorities appears to be required, then this may imply a change of leadership. The leadership thrown up in the first instance may be of people committed purely to one view of what the association should do or with talents that are most appropriate to the initial phase, such as charismatic individuals. It is not uncommon for groups at this stage of development to enter into overt conflict situations in which the early leaders are ejected from their position (Collison, 1963) or alternatively for a group to fail to change its leadership and begin to stagnate. This process has been analysed for community groups by Dennis (1961) and a similar relationship between change in function and leadership renewal has been noted in larger social movements (Gusfield, 1966).

A number of things will determine the ability of the community group to live through the crisis posed by a possible shift in function. An obvious one is the strength and solidarity of the core group. It should be self-confident. It should be able to see issues clearly and not get bogged down in procedure or rhetoric. It should have a skilled chairman. It should have a system of informal roles (such as clarifier of issues, gadfly, jester, conciliator) complementing the system of formal roles (such as chairman, treasurer, secretary). It should have a sense of group identity and solidarity built up by working together in the face of difficulties. It is also important that such group strength, as was said before, does not lead to a lack of contact with other actual and potential members of the organisation. A second prerequisite is active and involved support by a large proportion of the organisation's constituency. (This is presuming that one is talking about a fairly complex group rather than a small self-help or talk-out group of the sort often provided by Mothers In Action or People Not Psychiatry.) Such active support normally implies a high level of division of responsibility, frequent use of general meetings and a wide range of activity that will attract people with varying interests. A third feature that will help the community group in this crisis is the development of a group belief system (which may be borrowed from that of a broader social movement to which the group belongs, such as the Community Association and Claimants' Union movements). A purely ideological belief system may help in the short term. But one which more realistically appraises the position of the group will be better in the long run. This is why belief systems centring around the notion of 'community spirit' may be less productive of neighbourhood solidarity than ones based on shared but sectional interests (such as those of council tenants). 'Community' ideologies are particularly dangerous because they often imply a moral obligation on the part of people to join in community group activities and can be used to rationalise and justify the 'martyrdom complex'. The need for a group belief system to be realistic points to the final and probably most important factor in securing group survival through the crisis. This is the existence of real needs which the group is in a position to meet. They do not have to be the most important needs among the contact population. They may, in fact, be fairly trivial, such as the need for cheap and untaxing afternoon entertainment in the form of a modest bingo session. But they must be real. A group may survive with very little function except to cater to the pride and self-esteem of the core group. But it will not be a healthy one. An organisation that will really come through the crisis after the initial enthusiasm successfully is one that has a real purpose to serve, principles based on those purposes, the support of a significant part of the constituency and a strong core group that is aware of these other factors.

The community worker may have an important role to play during the crisis. He may be able to help the group to become more effective by acting as an interpreter in internal conflicts, though it requires great sensitivity to see just when one can do this. He should have remained sufficiently independent of the core group to be able to see ways in which they may be failing to secure the support of the constituency and may be able to point these out successfully. He may, because of his knowledge of other similar groups, be able to suggest functions and activities to the group which they had not considered. Above all, by the simple fact that he knows beforehand that this sort of crisis is likely to occur, by speaking about it and encouraging people to live through it, he may be able to diminish a good deal of the despondency and unrealistic internal conflict it is likely to generate. This does not mean that his role becomes one of merely enabling the group to function as a group that satisfies its members. On the contrary, his role should be to help the group re-define its function clearly. Only if it does this successfully is it likely to remain or to become a group that is satisfactory to its members. Above all, the worker must avoid as far as possible becoming a partisan in internal quarrels if he is to remain effective. And he must certainly avoid becoming so closely tied in with a core group that he is unable to criticise them constructively and unable to assist new initiatives in the contact population which may be helpful.

This role of interpreter to the group of its own progress is not the worker's only one even in this phase. Much of his time may be taken up with making practical suggestions, arranging contacts, giving information or providing resources. But, if the group does go through a critical stage such as that described after the initial burst of enthusiasm, then these other, more task-oriented roles must inevitably be subordinate to that of the outsider who helps the group understand its own development.

Once a group has gone through this crisis, it is likely to settle into some sort of routine. If the functions of the group are fairly limited, this may continue almost indefinitely. But, if it is wide in function, the routine is likely to be disturbed in a number of ways.

It may be disturbed by a new grievance. A long established Tenants' Association may be faced with a large rent increase and the possibility of turning once more into a mainly campaigning body with consequent changes in priorities, structures and possibly leadership. Here the community worker may have an important role in helping the group to clarify what changes are necessary and to what extent there is real continuity.

Alternatively, a crisis may be created by the availability of new resources, either through the group's own efforts or through grant aid. There are many possible resources, but one of the most important would be a building. A social or information centre is a significant addition to the resources of a neighbourhood organisation or community group. It poses fresh problems of administration within the group. The management of the building can become a major concern to the extent that the group exists to serve the building rather than the reverse. Activities which do not require the building may be neglected. Those which do need the building, and especially those that raise money that can be used to maintain the building, may be over-appreciated. People, particularly young people, who damage the building may attract the hostility of the core group. If an authority has contributed in any way to the building, there may be conflict over management powers which is not only damaging in itself, but may distract attention from more important issues of conflict between the community group and that authority. There may be an important role for the community worker in helping the group to clarify the functions of the building and the demands it makes and to come to a satisfactory agreement over management with the providing authority.

A third source of disturbance to routine may be contact with other groups. If this is with groups that are similarly routinised, the disturbance may not be very great. But in some crises there may be attempts to draw the group into new local social movements. There may also be problems if a group wishes to undertake a certain task, the success of which requires their co-operation with other groups to which they have a certain antipathy that makes them reluctant to co-operate where this is possible without surrender of principle. It may be part of the function of a community worker to introduce groups to specific social movements to which they might belong and help them to be realistic about the possible gains to them in co-operating with other groups in a variety of ways.

A fourth form of disturbance should come from the community worker himself, if for some reason he remains in fairly close contact with a group for more than a few months or if he makes contact with an established group. When a community worker has been in on the formation of a group he has probably gone with them through the process of defining objectives and designing structures. He may as a result be in danger of narrowing his own perspectives and of viewing what is as the possible. This would be a disservice to the group. One of his major functions as an outsider should be to feed in new ideas. The work of analysing the situation of the area or contact population is not one that is finished when the group is established. It should be on-going and he should be alive to changes in the contact population that suggest that changes in the group are needed.

Of course, for various reasons a group may die. It may be that it has served its purpose. There may be a lack of resources to continue work. The group may fold up through internal weaknesses. If a community group does die, it is as well to give it a decent burial. There is a great danger that people will be left feeling that the experience was not worth while, that 'it's useless trying to start anything around here'. It may be valuable for the group to wind up formally with an appreciation of what it has been able to achieve, quite apart from the fact that the existence of funds may make a formal dissolution necessary. But the burial should be a decent one. Maudlin sentimentality about what a Good Thing the group was may lead to a guilt-prompted suggestion that it be revived when really it has no hope of survival and the fresh start merely prolongs the death agony. Again, the role of the community worker here is to clarify issues and help people face pleasant and unpleasant facts and to learn from them.

The role of the community worker and elements in the worker/contact relationship

What has been said about the role of the community worker may prompt a number of questions.

1. The first is whether community workers are needed at all. Much of this chapter has been taken up with things that a community group must do in order to grow and develop. The suggestion that the community worker can clarify, encourage, mediate or inform has been tagged on almost as an afterthought.

It is true that many community groups start quite spontaneously and never need the help of a community worker, or need it only in the very restricted form of, for example, specific information about some point of law or administrative procedure. But there are many groups which for one reason or another need to be helped by community workers, or at least operate more effectively when they receive such help. The mere presence of a community worker can produce movement in a situation because it is evidence to people who have felt neglected in the past that someone takes their problems seriously. And the worker may be able to help in a

THE DEVELOPMENT OF COMMUNITY GROUPS

number of other ways that have been indicated.

2. A second question might concern the roles played by the worker. In very general terms there appear to be two main roles—that of initiating collective action and that of assisting it. The existence of the former role constitutes one of the major differences between most casework and most community work, for the caseworker usually has the client referred to him (by the client himself or another person or agency) and plays no part in initiating the relationship, whereas the community worker often is responsible for initiating the worker/contact relationship. These two basic roles may be subdivided again in fairly general terms:

1. Initiator of activity:
   (a) Researcher and analyser of situations.
   (b) Provider of service (e.g. adventure playground, advice centre) which provides base for contact with population.
   (c) Agitator (not necessarily in a militant sense); the role of bringing people together to discuss possibilities for collective action.

2. Assistant in activity:
   (a) Service role (e.g. community centre warden).
   (b) Role of giving advice and information on law and administration or techniques (e.g. in community television, play leadership, organising demonstrations) or on specific local situations.
   (c) Interpreter of group to itself, enabling it to develop in useful ways and avoid unnecessary internal conflict or inefficiency.
   (d) Mediator (between the group and statutory bodies or other community groups).

Not all these roles will be necessary in all situations. Many community workers would be suspicious of colleagues who adopted roles (2) (a) and (2) (d) too easily, feeling that this can create an undesirable dependency. Many again would be able to work in situations where initiatory roles (1) would not be necessary, since there was a good deal of spontaneous or established activity. Several, possibly all, of the roles mentioned could be further subdivided and made more specific. Or, again, they could all be summarised in terms of a single role—that of helping people to undertake collective action—which might be qualified in terms of values and long-term objectives of the sort dealt with in chapter 2.

3. A third question might be one about the 'style' of the com-

munity worker. He has been described as going out of his way to form judgments about areas and problems, to meet the people concerned without there having been any initiative on their part, to raise issues with them, to suggest lines of action and to participate in committee meetings, public meetings and other group activities in a fairly active way. To many social caseworkers this looks like a highly directive approach which offends against their social work principles.

Some of the questions of principle raised by this sort of query have been dealt with briefly in chapter 2. What might be useful here would be to point out some of the differences of work situation between the caseworker and the community worker.

The caseworker is often a figure of authority or may be seen (however inaccurately) by the client as having resources at his disposal that the client needs. The interviews often take place in neutral surroundings that allow for a fair degree of concentration. All this makes it possible for the caseworker to have a great deal of power in the one-to-one situation and social workers have been quite right to be worried about their use of it. Of course, this is only one aspect of the situation and is far from true of all social caseworkers all of the time. Nevertheless, the contrast with the work situation of the majority of community workers is there. Community workers are normally without authority and frequently without resources other than their own skills. They make their initial contacts with the people with whom they work very often without any initiative on the part of those people and the work is normally done in the contacts' territory. This means that they have to project themselves, allow their own personalities to be evident, in order to establish a relationship, being less able to depend on formal roles. This need not involve highly extrovert behaviour. It may imply merely that, for example, they demonstrate themselves to be highly reliable and consistent in the early stage of a project in order to reassure the contacts that they are serious. But some situations do require extrovert behaviour. A good deal of community work is done at public meetings, demonstrations, social events and in other situations where there is considerable 'noise' in the sense in which that term is used in communications theory and, perhaps, quite literally. Loud and forceful speaking in an emotionally-charged public meeting can be the equivalent in intent and effect to a quietly worded query in a one-to-one interview.

It is, of course, possible to manipulate groups. But there are limits to this if one has influence and not power. Most techniques of group manipulation require at least two people. Thus, if the connection between them is known, two allies can play the roles of Nice and Nasty and employ these to elicit responses which are emotional rather than rational. Or, if the group does not know of the connection between them, one can support the suggestions of the other at a crucial stage and thereby give the impression that the meeting is tending to agree with him and thus help to produce the desired effect. But these techniques cannot be used by the isolated community worker and they are short term in their results. In the heady atmosphere of a crowded meeting or a demonstration it is sometimes possible to persuade people to agree to the most extraordinary things. But, once the group pressure is lifted, they are likely to return to a more normal attitude. One of the justifications offered for highly aggressive demonstrations in the days of the Vietnam Solidarity Campaign was that, if a liberally-minded demonstrator was pushed around by an exasperated policeman in the course of such an event, he would, as a result, be 'politicised', that is to say, would accept revolutionary ideas. Some such conversions did appear to take place, but many more people who went through the experience decided to steer clear of such situations in the future. Manipulation that is long term in effect is normally only possible in a negative sense. One can introduce such confusion into a situation that no decision is made and this can discourage future activity. A common way of doing this is to press for a vote on an issue and after the vote produce a bizarre interpretation or several conflicting interpretations of the decision thus made. But community workers are usually involved in helping people to take up rather than drop initiatives so that, morality apart, this sort of technique is not really open to them.

In general it can be presumed that anything like conscious manipulation would not only be avoided on grounds of principle but would be fairly difficult to manage in practice.

Fears that the work styles of community workers are indications that manipulation is taking place probably reflect to some extent the highly individualistic approach to group situations that is common in this country, as in other parts of the Anglo-Saxon world. Groups tend to be seen both by casual observers and in the methodological nominalism of most group dynamics studies as fields in which largely autonomous individuals seek gains, whether by co-operation or conflict. This bias is evident in a good deal of the terminology used (such as 'leadership bid'). It underrates both empirically and normatively the experience of group solidarity. The community worker is not, or should not be, an outsider getting what he can out of a group situation, but someone attempting to pick up the potentialities of the group, its own possibilities for achievement.

Conclusion

The emphasis in this chapter has been on the community worker as the interpreter of the community group to itself. Many community workers would reject such an emphasis, fearing precisely that it could lead to manipulation. They would prefer to emphasise what one might call the 'agitator' and 'civil servant' aspects of the community worker role, seeing the worker as an expert in certain areas of policy (e.g. planning) or technical skill (e.g. journalism) rather than an expert in the ways the groups themselves work. There is clearly a good deal to be said for this point of view. Certainly there is a need in community work training and literature for more serious thought to be given to the wide range of technical skills that the job can involve. But it seems to me that to be successful at all the community worker must have skills in dealing with group situations and it makes little difference to the issue of principle whether these skills are acquired half-consciously by experience or more consciously by training and reflection. Moreover, a focus on the community worker's role in relation to the groups with which he works may help to give a clearer picture of what community workers actually do, which is one of the intentions of this book. The next chapter, which is mainly concerned with recording and evaluation, may also help to give a clearer picture of one type of community work involvement.

5

Recording and evaluation

Introduction

Community work is expensive in time, money and resources. Because of this, it requires evaluation and this brings in the issue of record-keeping.

Many community workers are hostile to, or at least dubious about, the idea of recording their work. Their relationship with the people with whom they work is normally on an egalitarian basis which seems to be undermined if conversations are written up later. Moreover, the worker is not dealing with individual cases whose records may need to be handed on to other workers or used for preparing reports for various authorities or professional colleagues. Often enough the worker is operating for some time in a fairly small area and can keep most of the salient facts in his memory.

My own viewpoint is that the keeping of certain records, particularly in the early stages of a project, is a very useful form of self-discipline, enabling one to understand the development of the project more clearly. There is also a strong need now, when community work is developing in new directions, for serious evaluation. Unless there is some discipline in recording, post-project evaluation becomes more difficult, even if the participants are still around to be questioned. The reader can consult the comments on this issue in Mitton and Morrison (1972). There is also the fact that a large number of community work agencies are not neighbourhood based, but are dealing over longer periods with large numbers of groups. Such agencies may need records purely as records. The point about the discrepancy between the egalitarian relationship and secret recording is taken. But the justification for recording remains and it need not be secret. Some community workers have experimented successfully with using their records as a basis for discussion with the leaders of the groups described in the records.

Most of this chapter is taken up with describing one pattern of recording that might be employed. It is not a standard pattern and might be highly inappropriate for many community work situations. The reader might find it useful to compare what is said here with the chapter on recording in Dunham (1958). The pattern of recording that is described in this chapter is illustrated with examples. These refer to a project that has been invented for the purposes of this chapter and neither the group nor the agency concerned really exists. The fictitious project is that of a new worker in a central community work agency in a large city who assists a council estate Tenants' Association during the first six months or so of its life. The illustrations are simply that, and should not be taken as models of all that good recording should be, nor should the work they describe be presumed to be free of fault.

Neighbourhood analysis

It is probably useful if, soon after starting work in an area (say, one month, if the work is likely to last for six months to a year), the worker puts on paper his impressions of the contact population. Such a report is roughly equivalent to an 'initial diagnosis' document in casework and should help to clarify ideas about possible courses of action. It may also be helpful to refer back to it later to see what problems that struck one initially one has later neglected or were incorrectly assessed. The starting point for such a report should be a statement of the reasons why the project was started. These considerations should govern to a large extent, though not exclusively, the sort of information offered. By and large (and assuming one's contact population is that of a small area and not a special interest group or grouping of organisations) the sort of issues covered in the report should be:

(a) The boundaries of the area.
(b) Land usage in it.
(c) Class and other social characteristics of the residents.
(d) Age structure.
(e) Population mobility.
(f) Amenities.

(g) Local organisations and leaders.

(h) Social problems.

(i) Illustrative incidents or comments from those in the area.

(This check list is based on that suggested in Leaper, 1971.)

This is a good deal with which to cope and obviously the worker will have to limit himself to what he can do in a short period of time in which he will also be making relationships and starting his actual work. Such a report would be an initial assessment and not a piece of sociological research. If one can obtain precise figures easily, well and good. If not, it is probably not a priority. Because the worker needs to know and be known in the area, it is probably as useful for him to pick up gossip in the pub or launderette as to be able to draw a precise diagram of the population's age structure. It is only when claims are made that a social problem is noticeably absent or prevalent in an area that it may be useful to go out of one's way to attempt to discover precise figures. Even if commonly held beliefs about an area are shown to be false, however, the fact that they are commonly held is still important and the worker needs to consider why this is so.

Whole books have been written about small neighbourhoods or special interest groups. Here again it is important for the worker to realise the limits of this sort of exercise and write something comparatively brief in which the more important points are highlighted.

The initial report should be written as an aid to future action and it is those points that are relevant to such action that should be brought out most clearly. (In the example that follows potential conflicts within the committee are emphasised.) The report should end with suggested provisional objectives for the project.

Neighbourhood report: the Windmill Estate Windmill Estate lies to the north of the city in a residential area consisting mainly of local authority housing built at different periods. It is in fairly hilly country well to the north of the main industrial belt which means that there is some difficulty for people travelling to work, but also that, as one of the residents put it to me, 'It's like the country here, with fresh air and that.'

The estate has been built on what had been private parkland up until its donation to the authority in the will of the last owner. The central piece of the park has been retained and a number of tower blocks and semis built around it. Though the dwellings are

85

pretty unimaginative in their exterior design, any monotony is more than offset by the way they have been sited. The estate has, in fact, some prestige status and this may be reflected in the fact that two or three tenants with whom I spoke blamed children from the nearby 1930s 'cottage estate' of Riverbrook for the few acts of vandalism that have occurred.

I get the impression that it is the 'better class' of applicant that has been offered houses on Windmill. I may have been over-impressed by the fact that a couple of the members of the Tenants' Association committee are more 'middle class' than I would have expected council tenants to be. But Mrs Simms, the Housing Welfare Officer, whom I saw at the department, said: 'We have been very selective on the Windmill Estate.'

The estate is still in the process of construction, though almost all the dwellings completed are now occupied. Because building is not entirely completed, tenants have to cope with mud, heavy vehicles used by the builders, and the fact that only one shop has opened (a newsagent which, for the time being at least, is also acting as something of a general stores). Until a week ago there was no bus service for the estate as such, although some 1,500 dwellings are planned and more than a thousand are now complete and occupied. There were and are fairly frequent buses along the nearby Northbank Road, but getting to them involved quite a trek for the people living at the further end of the estate. There is a primary school which serves a wider area than the new estate. It is called the John Morris School (after the donor of the land). The Orange-tree Comprehensive is within reasonable distance.

Those tenants with whom I have spoken are irritated by the grievances I have indicated, but on the whole are proud to be on a 'prestige' estate and are pleased with their new homes.

The Windmill Estate was referred to the agency by the Rev. Mr Ainsworth on the advice of Mr Chumley, the Housing Manager. A group of women on the estate, including a Mrs Jones, had got together after gossiping in the newsagent's about various amenity problems on the estate. They had sent a deputation to the Housing Manager who had promised to take up the issues they raised. He seems to have persuaded Transport to put on a new bus service earlier than they had intended. He also put it to the group that they would meet problems with which they could deal in a self-help manner and might like to form an Association. He suggested that Mr Ainsworth at the already existing Anglican church of St

Philomena's might let them use his parish hall for a public meeting. Such a meeting was called two months ago and the Association was formed with Mrs Jones as secretary and a Mr Smith as chairman. Mr Ainsworth, after consulting his parish church council and the bishop, suggested that he might be able to lease the hall to the Association freely and indefinitely, if they would assume responsibility for running expenses. This may be an ambiguous gift as the hall is in some state of disrepair. But there seem to be no major structural faults.

Since being formed, the Association has fairly successfully taken up a number of grievances with the local authority. Arrangements are being made for a small old people's lunch club to be held in the church hall. A playgroup has started, though it is experiencing difficulty and is seriously under-equipped. There is talk of having a Youth Night, but also some opposition to this. There are fairly definite plans for a boys' football team and one local man is prepared to organise art classes. All this activity is centred on the hall, although the matter of the lease has not yet been settled. Subscriptions of 1p a week are raised and the collection of these gives the committee members a chance to meet people on the estate, including a few isolated elderly people. Although this is hard, time-consuming work, they seem willing to do it.

My first contact was with Mr Smith, whom Mr Ainsworth took me to meet. At Mr Smith's invitation I attended a committee meeting two days later. I have tried to see as many committee members as possible and they mostly seem happy to accept my help. I have also met people at the Housing Department and Social Services. The school seems uninterested in any contact. I have helped actively in the arrangements for the lunch club and in the running of the playgroup. I have used the pub and the newsagent's as places in which to get into conversations with people not on the committee.

The committee itself is a body with a lot of potential internal conflict, but also with a great deal of talent and some previous organisational experience. Officially there are sixteen members, excluding Mr Ainsworth who is 'honorary'. Of these about a dozen seem to be fairly involved and half a dozen form the leadership core.

Mr Smith, the chairman, is a rather nervous looking man. He has had experience as secretary of his works social club and is ambitious to make the WETA hall into a well-equipped social centre with a big financial turnover. He has put a lot of work into planning how this might be done. He is very conservative in his opinions, though not in the least politically active. On both these counts he is suspicious of those in the WETA whom he calls 'highly motivated'. I find some embarrassment in the fact that he expects me to be on his side, especially as at the one meeting I have attended so far he was ineffectively authoritarian as chairman.

Mrs Jones, the secretary, appears older than she is. From comments she made about her past life I gather that she is in her late forties. She is a devout Roman Catholic and—in spite of her husband's name—Irish. She sometimes talks about the fact that her uncle was put in prison before the war for being in the IRA, which does nothing to make her popular on the estate. She appears to have had a tough upbringing in a working-class, left-wing household. She was expelled from the Labour Party for leading a rent strike two years ago. That she should be accepted for this estate suggests either deviousness or an administrative slip up on the part of the lettings section or perhaps merely that the selection process is not as rigorous as the housing welfare officer suggested. She was anxious to meet me and test out my opinions. Her attitude is that 'he that is not with us is against us' and it would be easy to make an enemy of her.

Mr Shearer, the treasurer, is a small, neatly-dressed wages clerk in his forties. He has acted as treasurer to a number of small groups in the past. Apart from his ability in this field, he also has a good sense of humour and relieved one difficult situation at the committee meeting with an appropriate joke.

Mrs Hobdell, a student teacher, is a young divorced woman with a two-year-old son. She is working class in background and 'has no nonsense about her' as one of the other women put it. She is officially responsible for the playgroup, but cannot always be there.

Mrs Seabrook is a young mother of three children who is, I suspect, a highly intelligent woman who has missed out on her education. She is the effective leader of the playgroup and, I think, a little jealous of Mrs Hobdell.

Mr Loughton is a skilled manual worker and for a long time was a keen member of the Territorial Army. He is going to organise the football team and annoys some by insisting that a 'decent strip' and other equipment be purchased as soon as possible, though he is supported in this by Mr Smith.

Mrs Rein is another member of the Catholic parish. She is a mildly spoken lady who does a lot of home visiting. She has been put in charge of the lunch club project, but is a bit bewildered by the bureaucratic preliminaries.

Mr Birch is a pensioner, rather garrulous about his long experience in working men's clubs, but a hard worker.

Mrs Macmillan is a grey-haired lady who is always extremely well dressed. She says little, but seems at committee meetings to be in a mood of constant disapproval.

Mr Hall is a young married man without children. He works in a bank and has some kind of position in his trade union. His views are left wing, but not apparently of any one party or political group. Mrs Jones is very ambivalent about him. She realises that he is a possible ally, but she suspects him of being a member of the Communist Party, to which she is virulently opposed. As far as I can make out, this is not the case.

Mr Ainsworth, the vicar, is a slightly cynical man in his forties. I feel he wishes to hand over the hall mainly because he sees no prospect of its being used by his dwindling parish. Mrs Simms, the Housing Welfare Officer, is a rather snappy bureaucrat who is suspicious of the Association, though I do not think she will actively interfere. Mr Chumley, the Housing Manager, seemed to me charming and well-intentioned, but rather authoritarian underneath it all. He wanted me to encourage a gardening club for the tenants in the semis on the estate. He is presumably encouraging the Association because he sees that sort of thing as being part of good housing management and hopes that, if it is successful, it will further enhance the prestige of the estate and thus of his department.

I think my main tasks may be to help sort out any conflict between Mrs Smith and Mrs Jones and to rescue the Youth Night which may be established from the well-drilled Lads' Club routine which Mr Loughton would like to impose. Meanwhile I will try to help the lunch club and the playgroup through their initial difficulties because this will be useful to them and should help to establish my position with the committee.

On-going recording

While the worker is engaged on his project he should keep brief day-to-day records of his activity. These should include information, not only on any lengthy contacts he has with particular individuals or on any meetings he attends, but also on more casual contacts with people in the area, social activities at which he is present and contacts with officials and other relevant people outside the area itself. It is important that all these things be noted as all of them can contribute to the success of the project. They should be as consistent in form as is compatible with the variety of contacts. The amount of detail included depends on what is considered relevant. One might simply note something such as:

> Evening: Met Mr Smith in pub. Talked about progress in getting old people's lunch club arranged. Said I would meet him at the next meeting.

But notes of this sort are likely to mean little to anyone other than the worker concerned. They suffice to indicate the kind of contact he has maintained with some of the individuals with whom he is working. But in some contacts which are fairly casual, significant comments may be made which illustrate features of the situation or even help to develop it, and these need to be recorded in some detail. For example:

> Evening: Met Mr Smith in pub. I talked about the progress of the negotiations over the old people's lunch club. He told me: 'The reason why there's been all this delay, you know, is because the Corporation know that Mrs Jones is our secretary and she's a well-known trouble maker. I didn't want her elected on to the committee really. She started that rent strike two years ago and she'd like to get rid of me because I'm in her way. She's why the Town Hall won't let us have the lunch club!' I tried to point out some of the reasons why this was not likely to be so, that it was Social Services, not Housing, that was responsible for the lunch club, that Mr Chumley had supported the Association even though he knew that Mrs Jones was involved and that the indications coming from Social Services were that the lunch club would be settled in a couple of months because it fitted in with their plans anyway. All this was said in bits and pieces in a two-way conversation lasting several minutes. But Mr Smith seemed less interested in the lunch club than in his complaints about Mrs Jones.

He has said this sort of thing before, but never so vehemently. It was obvious that by challenging what he was saying I was merely arousing his antagonism, so I let it drop. I said I would be at the next meeting.

This particular example indicates that, not only did the worker fail to cope with the situation at the time, but he had not really considered ways of dealing with it in future, as he has not mentioned anything of this sort. Had things been slightly better handled and had the process of recording been used to reconsider the situation, the latter part of the recording might have run:

But Mr Smith seemed less interested in the lunch club than in his complaints about Mrs Jones. I let him talk for some time and then tried to reassure him that the rest of the committee would never allow a single person to take over the Association (a double-edged comment, perhaps, but it was not meant as such at the time). I avoided complicity in his condemnation of Mrs Jones. I decided in my own mind to be alert to any indications from other committee members that they feel, as I am beginning to do, that Mr Smith is unreasonable about Mrs Jones and blocks complaints coming from tenants because he under-estimates Mr Chumley's ability to keep his cool about that sort of thing. I switched the discussion to what could be achieved by the Association in the next few months with the playgroup and other activities as well as the lunch club. I said I would be at the next meeting.

An extract from the day-to-day record notes on a project might run something like:

Tuesday 5th. As arranged at the committee meeting last night I went to see Mrs Rein in the morning. She gave me the information relating to the lunch club and I said I would see what I could do.

In the afternoon, back at the office, I rang Mrs Kelley at Social Services. She said she thought there would be no difficulty over the lunch club and offered to see me on Friday at 10.30 in her office.

Friday 8th. Saw Mrs Kelley at her office. She showed me

the file on Windmill and said that a club had been planned
in that area in any case. There was always a delay in
setting up these things even though the department had a
very active policy in this field, but, because one had
been planned before the request came from the WETA and
because of the offers of local help coming through the
Association, everything should get going in a couple of
months. She quite understood people's impatience with
the procedure and said she would be willing to come to a
committee meeting to explain in person if it would help. As
we may have further contact with Mrs Kelley in relation
to other neighbourhoods I spent some time discussing lunch
clubs in general with her (report in Social Services
Department file).

In the afternoon I walked round the estate again. Met Mrs
Jones in the newsagent's. She said that she had wanted to
see me. She described her political background (uncle
used to be a member of the IRA, she herself was expelled
from the Labour Party for starting a rent strike two years
ago). She questioned me about my views. I indicated
that in general they were in sympathy with hers.

Called on Mrs Rein, Mr Shearer, Mrs Smith (message for her
husband) and Mr Ainsworth to arrange an informal
meeting about the lunch club leaflet on Monday evening.
Monday 11th. Spent most of the day walking around the
estate. Spoke to some people at the bus stop who
complained about the new bus service and about the
difficulty of getting old furniture into the flats. I gathered they
were recent arrivals. They had not heard about the
Association and I gave them some details. Two of them
gave me their names and addresses for Mrs Jones.

Meeting in evening settled question of the leaflet to tell
elderly people on the estate about progress with the
lunch club (copy attached).
Tuesday 12th. Did leaflet in morning and took copies to
Mrs Rein. Spent afternoon at playgroup, not very
effectively as the women seemed dubious about a man in
that setting.
Friday 15th. Tried unsuccessfully to obtain an appointment
with the primary school headmaster. Spent lunch time in
pub chatting with a group of older men. One said that the

WETA was a clique, but others disagreed, apparently because they have a high opinion of Mrs Rein and the work that she does.

Process recording

When a conversation is recorded in some detail, then one is approaching what in social casework is called process recording. Just as process recording is used extensively in social work for training purposes or for helping a worker in difficulty to clarify his thinking about a particular situation, so similar types of recording can be employed in community work settings. The discussion with Mr Smith described above would be an incident that might be recorded in that way.

In community work process recording need not be confined to one-to-one situations. It may be useful for a worker or student to process record a meeting of some kind or certain types of group activity, such as playgroup sessions and demonstrations.

An important consideration in recording meetings either for on-going records or in process recording is that the worker's purpose in recording is not that of a group secretary. The secretary of a group or committee or organisation adopts a formal tone in writing minutes because he is trying to record policy decisions unambiguously. The worker's purpose in recording is to help himself and others to understand the group. Therefore the formal tone of official minutes is inappropriate.

In one sense process recording many group events is easier than recording one-to-one sessions in casework. The worker is not necessarily so closely involved in the discussion. It is easier, therefore, for him to observe. In another sense it is more difficult, since there is more to observe. If ten people are gathered together there are 45 possible one-to-one relationships. In a public meeting with two hundred people present there are 19,000 possible one-to-one relationships. Of course, in practice the complexity is reduced by the fact that people's personalities are only partly, often very superficially, involved and that they respond to the rest of the group as a whole or to a few leading figures. Nevertheless, the complexity exists which makes an analytical structure for recording necessary.

Social psychologists have devised a number of methods of recording group processes which consist essentially of categorising each intervention made and producing statistical/narrative descriptions of the process on that basis. While this sort of analysis can often reveal aspects of a group that might otherwise have escaped attention, it is rarely advisable to attempt even simplified forms of this kind of recording in community work settings. It is difficult to keep the necessary detailed notes during a meeting. The method records only how the group worked as a group and does not place it in its setting. It may be necessary to analyse very closely the roles of particular individuals or sub-groups as a guide to follow-up action.

Approaches to process recording in casework situations offer probably the most useful basis for approaches to similar recording of group events. Adapting some of the existing widely used guidelines for casework process recording, one might suggest a structure for group process recording along the following lines:

1. Purpose of the group event and of the worker in attending.
2. Observations about the group members and setting.
3. Content:
    (a) A description of how the meeting, social session, etc. began.
    (b) Pertinent factual information about decisions taken and reasons for them or of other activity according to the type of group event and the responses of the group members and of the worker to these things.
    (c) A description of the feeling content of the group event on the part of the members, the worker and any other outsiders.
    (d) Notes on how the event ended and, in particular, whether it was on an optimistic note or a pessimistic one and whether any necessary decisions had been firmly made and arrangements finalised to ensure that they would be put into effect.
4. Impressions on a more general level.
5. A brief summary of the worker's role in the events, outlining how far this was thought out and followed decisions taken by him before the event.
6. Plan of future action.

In any case of recording a group process in a community work setting and especially in a process record the worker is concerned with four main things:

1. Did the group session achieve its purpose (e.g. carry out an

activity successfully, arrive at clear decisions, etc.)?
2. What was the feeling of the meeting like? Did things run smoothly? Was there an atmosphere of co-operation and interdependence? How did the group cope with any internal conflict? Was it suppressed or resolved, or brought out into the open but not resolved?
3. What were the different roles of individual people in the group? Were there any who contributed notably to making things go well or badly, and, if so, how? Were there any silent, retiring members of the group?
4. What was the worker's role? (Even if he maintained silence throughout, he would still need to explain in the recording why he did so and how this contributed to the development of events.)

It is sometimes apparently felt that only meetings or at least more or less organised discussions can be recorded. This reflects an over-intellectual approach to group interaction which sees it basically in terms of articulated exchange. Partly for this reason, the example of group process recording given below is of a play-group session. (This is the one noted briefly in the project notes quoted above for Tuesday 12th, early on in the project.)

WETA playgroup session The Association's playgroup meets twice a week—Tuesday afternoon and Thursday morning. In each case the session lasts just under two hours (as the group is not a registered one) in the church hall. The days were chosen to fit in with the times Mrs Hobdell is at the moment free on her course. But, in fact, she is so busy in college that often she is not at the playgroup. Effective control seems to be in the hands of Mrs Seabrook, another committee member. I had gathered something of this situation before I went to this session of the playgroup.

I asked if I could go to the session, partly to complete my information on WETA activities, partly to see if I could help in any way and thus do something to establish my position in the group.

When I arrived there were four mothers present and about a dozen children, including Brendan Hobdell, but not his mother. Three of the mothers were in different parts of the room, each playing with or watching over a small group of children. One had books and some painting equipment, another bricks and other small toys, a third two rather battered play cars. Children drifted from group to group as they felt like it, while the three mothers stayed where they were. Mrs Seabrook was busy doing some kind of paper work. I introduced myself by asking whether she remembered me from the meeting and saying that Mrs Hobdell had invited me to the playgroup session. She did remember me, but did not appear to welcome my intrusion.

I asked her about the running of the playgroup. At first this brought a stream of complaints about the premises, the lack of equipment and the lack of willing helpers. Four people seemed a reasonable number to me, but it was obvious from her tone that the last was the sorest point as far as she was concerned. However, as she warmed to the subject, she became more enthusiastic. Whispering, she pointed out one little girl who, she said, had 'come on wonders' since joining the group. She made several comments on how useful it was for both the mothers and children to be able to get together, especially those who lived in the flats. In reply to a question she said she did not live in a tower block and had no intention of ever doing so.

I felt that Mrs Seabrook did not want to spend the whole time in conversation with me. She was making a great thing of her paper work which seemed to consist of little more than the totting up of some figures about refreshments and subscriptions to the playgroup. I think she was emphasising her role as unacknowledged leader by doing this sort of thing at the playgroup itself. In any case, after about fifteen minutes I went off to play with the children who were using the two play cars. After a while I realised that the woman who had been with this group of children had drifted off to talk with Mrs Seabrook. The group of children round me began to grow in number and none was left with the woman responsible for books and paints. She in turn went to ask Mrs Seabrook for a light and stayed talking to her. I began to get a bit panicky in case things got out of hand. I could see that two small boys were shaping up for a scrap. But in the meantime one of the women with Mrs Seabrook had put the kettle on. Mrs Seabrook announced that it was time for drinks and the children were hustled into a circle and sat down on chairs to wait for the refreshments.

Tea and soft drinks with biscuits were served to the adults and children. I was trapped for a while in conversation with a little girl who wanted to know whether I was a policeman or a teacher.

Then the woman who had been in charge of the books began to tell a story. I went off with the other three women to the far end of the room to drink my cup of tea. The woman who had been in charge of the bricks asked me whether I had any children myself. I was a bit taken aback by her slightly aggressive tone and simply said, 'No'. I was congratulated with light-hearted cynicism and then there was a lull in the conversation. To break it I asked where the children's chairs had come from. The lady with the bricks said that Mrs Hobdell had persuaded the Education Department to part with some old chairs and other equipment. She went on to say how good Mrs Hobdell had been and how it was her idea to have the three centres to the group, based on the three types of toy and to end up with the drink, story and song time. I asked if there were regular helpers. The lady with the bricks said it had been Mrs Hobdell's idea that mothers should be able to bring their children and then those that were able to stay could be the volunteers. There was a rota system so that at least one mother would know that she was expected to stay for any one session. The only stipulation was that mothers should call back promptly to collect their children. The woman who had been in charge of the play cars said, 'She needed to arrange that with hardly ever being here herself.' The lady with the bricks said: 'She's alright, Alice Hobdell. She may be educated, but she's no nonsense about her.'

Fortunately, at that point the singing game came to an end. There was a brief period of activity in which extra drinks were handed out and other mothers began to arrive, including Mrs Hobdell who came up to speak to me. I said goodbye to her and Mrs Seabrook and the others, saying I would probably see them again soon.

Looking back on it, I think that in effect I made a hurried escape, because I could not think what to do about the problems that had been raised there and then.

My impressions of the group were that:

1. It potentially serves a useful function, although it may need more equipment if it is to develop and extend its routine. The interest the children expressed in me may have been a result of boredom with the existing toys and the way things are done at present.
2. There is obviously a conflict between Mrs Hobdell and Mrs Seabrook in which other mothers are involved and possibly a conflict between those mothers that often stay and those that always simply leave their children at the playgroup.
3. In spite of the problems the group has got off to a fair start.

I am not sure whether or not to attend future sessions. Whether it was the fact that I was new to the group, or a man, or connected with Mrs Hobdell, the reception was not altogether friendly. It would depend partly on which of those factors was the most important whether it would be worth while retaining a close contact. I feel I will have to decide either never to go again or to go fairly often. I think I will choose the latter because the situation merits some attention, presuming, that is, that they are prepared to have me there.

I may also try to raise with Mrs Hobdell, once I know her and the other people involved better, the possibility of her relinquishing her position to Mrs Seabrook. I think Mrs Hobdell would be quite reasonable about this. She seems worried herself about not being able to devote enough time to the group.

One long-term possibility would be to try to set up a group of men or boys, or women for that matter, who could build toys and other equipment for the playgroup, rather like the group our agency set up on the Ryman Estate. This would need at least one skilled person in charge.

Evaluation

At some stage in the work with the group the community worker will decide to withdraw. This may mean a near complete close of contact with the group. Alternatively, it may mean that the worker will simply stop seeing the group as frequently as he has done during the main period of activity. At the time of withdrawal there should be a closing report which as far as possible should attempt an evaluation. One could have a project that was one of action/research or one might have historiographical attempts to reconstruct the development of a project by consulting the records and participating individuals. We need more of this sort of thing and the Home Office Community Development Project is making a valuable contribution precisely by its emphasis on evaluation. What is under consideration here is something less ambitious, but still serious, an honest attempt by the worker concerned to sit back and look at what happened.

Such a report would open with re-examination of the objectives of the project. One would look at who was to have been helped, whether these were professionals who were involved or the people they served or hoped to serve in co-operation with the community worker. One would specify what were the interim objectives originally set for the project. These might be such things as examining needs in an area, establishing whether there might be local support for some particular activity or structure, securing changes in the administrative procedure of the local authority, bringing together a number of agencies or organisations for a joint project, or a number of other things. These interim objectives might involve fairly specific provisional objectives, such as to establish a playgroup or secure better information for people affected by a clearance scheme. But, as was stressed in the last chapter, any such objective would be merely provisional and one might worry if they had not been modified as a result of the increased interaction with the contact population. Any evaluation report would consider what had happened to any such provisional specific objectives and why.

The report might then go on to a narrative account of the project which clarified the process of development and brought the account up until the time of writing the report. The report might then consider who had been helped by the project. These people would fall into a number of groups. 1. those who had first asked for the intervention or assistance of the worker; 2. those who had learned new skills or developed in some other way through the worker's help, such as the committee members of a local organisation; 3. those who received a service they did not have before, such as the elderly people attending a club or residents whose bus service had been improved; 4. individuals with particular problems whom the worker had been able to help. One would need to distinguish these groups quite clearly unless they did overlap completely. This would be especially important if some conflict had developed between them, if, for example, the people who asked for the worker's intervention in the first instance were unhappy with what he had done, but most of the contact population were not.

The report should close with some kind of estimate of future developments.

Where possible, hard figures should be used in making any evaluation, though obviously these can give a false impression of precision in some circumstances. One obvious set of figures is that outlining how much money was spent and how it was spent. Other figures might provide comparisons of the situation before and after the project. But it is highly unlikely that one could get hold of really useful statistics of this sort unless the project involved research work that was designed to produce them (as in the project reported in Festinger and Kelley, 1951).

The reader might like to compare the format for final evaluation offered here with that suggested by the Community Work Group (1973).

The concluding report is the most important form of recording in many ways and is especially crucial where no standard forms of record are maintained in the agency.

Final report on the WETA project   The Windmill Estate Tenants' Association was referred to the agency by the local vicar Mr Ainsworth some six months ago, about one month after I first came here. I have maintained fairly close contact with them during that period, attending all committee meetings, helping them to organise various activities and generally having some contact with the group two or three days a week. The Association is now well on its feet and has come to the close of an important stage of its development with a satisfactory agreement about the management of the premises they have always used, the church hall of St Philomena's. I have discussed the matter with the leading members of the committee and we have agreed that there is no need for me to continue maintaining close contact with them. There was a sort of formal leave-taking at the last committee meeting. I have assured them that I would be ready to help in the future in any way that I could. I will presumably see something of them now and then, if only at meetings of the Community Groups Liaison Committee.

Windmill Estate is well known in the city. It lies to the north in the largely council estate residential area consisting of Orange-tree and Northbrook Wards. It is still in the process of construction, though the last dwelling should be completed in the next few months. There are both semis and tower blocks. The estate is fairly attractive in design, though lacking in some amenities. The tenants are, on the whole, of a slightly higher social status than most council tenants. It is a prestige estate. I think this is why the Housing Manager, Mr Chumley, was so anxious to help the Association to set up and has gone further out of his way to make concessions to them than to some of the other tenants' associations. It was, incidentally, he who recommended us to Mr Ainsworth. He obviously sees encouraging social activities as part of good management and probably hoped that a thriving community association would add to the prestige of Windmill and thus to that of his department. He also seems to have wanted the group to engage in a bit of social control, forcing people to keep their gardens tidy; as the Association is thinking of a gardens' competition for the semis, he may even have gained that point.

When I first met the committee members of the Association it was obvious that there was a good deal of talent, but also a lot of potential for internal conflict. Much of this focused around Mrs Jones, the secretary, and Mr Smith, the chairman. The Association had started as a result of grievances arising out of the newness of the estate. Probably because Mr Chumley was so amenable (he got them a new bus service among other things), the Association went through the mainly grievance stage very early. When it was set up it was explicitly as a multi-functional organisation. Mr Smith, who was elected chairman, was and is mainly concerned with recreational activities. He was at first rather unsure of himself in his role as chairman, tended to be authoritarian in a bit of a ham-fisted way, and was suspicious of Mrs Jones. She had not only organised the original deputation, but had a lot of experience in protest through her trade union experience and more recently through her role in the rent strike nearly three years ago for which she was thrown out of the Labour Party. Apart from conflicts between these two there were also difficulties between other members of the committee, notably Mrs Hobdell and Mrs Seabrook who between them were responsible for the playgroup.

The public meeting which led to the formal establishment of the WETA was held in the church hall, as all activities have been since. The vicar, with the approval of the appropriate authorities, wanted to lease the hall to the Association for at most a nominal rent if they would undertake maintenance. As the building was in some disrepair and need of decoration, this meant in effect a fairly heavy rent at first. Heating costs are also considerable. This problem has now been solved by an Education grant towards repairs under conditions which give Education some say in the running of the building, but not too much. At any rate, the group has had the premises from the start. They, therefore, managed to get a number of activities going. There were regular bingo socials. Grouse meetings were held from which complaints could be relayed to the local authority. A playgroup was organised. A lunch club, now in operation, was planned. A football club was started. A private art class uses the premises and has affiliated itself to the Association.

A Youth Night was planned, but is still shelved. More recently, the Association has developed its early regular leaflet into a full scale monthly community newspaper.

My overall objective when I first made contact with the Association was to help them in any way that I could to get going. In particular I thought that I could:

1. Help to prevent the potential conflict between Mr Smith and Mrs Jones from breaking out in any harmful way, particularly in any way that would lead the Association to drop its concern with tenants' issues.

2. Assist in setting up the Youth Night and, in particular, rescue it from domination by one rather authoritarian committee member who was interested.

3. Help the committee members concerned deal with the bureaucracy at Social Services in getting their old people's lunch club set up.

4. Help with the playgroup.

The last two objectives I saw in terms of helping me to establish myself in the area.

In retrospect, I think that these objectives were misplaced. They represent slight misinterpretations of what was going on which were coloured by the lack of sympathy I felt with some committee members and an over-estimation of what I could hope to achieve in a situation where people were making decisions effectively for themselves. It is with regard to the last two objectives and a fifth that cropped up later that I have achieved most.

As Mr Smith settled down in his role as chairman, he became more confident and competent and was able to make a better relationship with Mrs Jones. The two were brought closer together by the involvement of the WETA in the Community Groups Liaison Committee which was formed soon after I started work with the WETA. The Windmill group formed a sort of middle group in the Liaison Committee because they did both what the older Community Associations did and what the Tenants' Associations and Residents' Action Groups did. They tried to use this middle position to make a leadership bid. This aroused a certain amount of antagonism in which Mr Smith and Mrs Jones drew closer together in self-defence. I also think that, as Mr Smith learned that not all people were treated as politely by the Housing Department as he was and as some proposals from the Liaison Committee were turned down or lost in the machine, he began to sympathise more with Mrs Jones, though still remaining basically 'unpolitical'. I had just not anticipated such a development. I had also over-estimated the strength behind the moves to set up a Youth Night. The only really enthusiastic committee members were Mr Lough-ton, the authoritarian whose domination of any youth club I dreaded, and Mrs Hobdell. Other committee members were dubious about their ability to cope with a Youth Night (some anti-teenager feeling being expressed). In the event Mr Loughton was soon too involved in the boys' football team to want to spend time on any-thing else and Mrs Hobdell, a divorcee who has a young child and is a student teacher, also lacked enough time. She has very recently arranged for discussions between the committee and the youth service section of the Local Education Authority, so there may be further developments there.

But my main work was concerned with the lunch club and the playgroup. I was able to act as an intermediary between Social Services and the committee about the setting up of the club. This was useful, as the inevitable delay in getting it going was helping to produce tension inside the committee. I was also able to act as a sort of administrative assistant to Mrs Rein who is responsible for the club. She has a very good relationship with many of the old people on the estate, but she had little idea about the problems of organising the club in the first place. I took a fairly directive role here, which she seemed happy to accept, and now that the structure is there the club is apparently working very well under her general direction. Just under fifty people come to each weekly session and the atmosphere is always lively.

My reception by the mothers running the playgroup was frosty at first. This was partly because I was a man, but mainly because I was introduced into the situation by Mrs Hobdell who had antagonised some of the mothers by assuming formal responsibility for the group, but doing little of the actual work. She herself was worried about this and was easily persuaded to step down as leader. This enabled her to spend more time on what was to her a more congenial project of making soundings about a grant for the building which is now forthcoming. (She knows quite a few people in the youth and adult education sections of the Education Department socially.) I won the acceptance of Mrs Seabrook, who took over from Mrs Hobdell, by driving her in the agency van over to an auction where she picked up a lot of toys for the play-group cheaply, using money from a jumble sale and raffle she had organised. This put her fairly innocently one up on Alice Hobdell who had only managed to obtain some rather battered old equipment for the group. This, in turn, made her better disposed towards me. I started to join in discussions with Mrs Seabrook and one or two other mothers who regularly helped at the playgroup about ways of developing it. My role here was mainly one of asking the right questions as they had most of the ideas. At one such session my presence raised explicitly the question of the roles of the two sexes in relation to child care. This, in turn, led to their visit to the Women's Lib. centre in town. It is ironic that my one involvement with the WETA that had an explicit political element was not in relation to tenants' issues, which had been my main initial interest, but a 'social activity'. The playgroup leaders are now involved in the centre's campaign for a more positive policy on play provision by the authority.

The fifth objective I eventually set myself was to help the group get its community newspaper off the ground. This was an idea that came from committee members. But I saw it as useful because it would help them maintain contact with the local people, especially after they dropped their early scheme of collecting a weekly subscription. The first moves were to develop the leaflets they had been circulating which advertised activities. I had thought at first of helping in the production of the newspaper in much the same way as I had helped with setting up the lunch club. It was intended that the agency's printing services could be used. But, after discussion with other workers at the agency, I thought it would be better if the group learned how to set up the paper by discussing it with those other community groups that had their own papers. There were two reasons for this. One was that there was a danger of creating a dependency on me if I went on doing the sort of thing I had done with the lunch club where it was unnecessary. The other was that this was an additional reason why the WETA should be involved in the Liaison Committee which it was agency policy to support. The WETA committee agreed with me when I put it to a committee meeting that it would be best for them to learn from groups with existing papers through the Liaison Committee. They themselves, soon after joining the Liaison Committee, suggested setting up a sort of mutual education group on papers, leaflets and posters. This was the group in which David McKie from the graphic design school at the polytechnic was involved. He picked up the fact that Windmill had a private art class and pointed out how useful this could be in producing attractive stuff when they had access to reasonably professional and cheap printing facilities. They took his point and the man who ran the art class agreed to help. This also helped to bring his group closer into the Association. (There had been some minor arguments about the use of the hall up until then.)

I think a large number of people have been helped by the WETA. It has successfully pursued a number of grievances, mainly over the bus service and the speed of construction. It has helped the new residents to settle into the area quickly and make friends. The lunch club and the playgroup and even the football club (in the absence of any other amenities for young people) are services which a number of people are using and for which they are grateful. Some people seem to have gained a good deal personally out of it. Mrs Seabrook is one such person. She has learned a lot about her own abilities, not only through running the playgroup, but through discussions the mothers have had. Mr Smith has also gained something. Although he has had a lot of previous experience with works clubs, this is the first time he has been chairman of a neighbourhood group. The setting is rather different and he seemed to find it difficult to adapt to it at first, but he is much more relaxed in the role now.

My own contribution, as has been explained, has been principally with the lunch club and the playgroup. My role has been to provide expertise where it was needed (particularly in setting up the lunch club), to help in the easing of one instance of leadership renewal (in the playgroup) and to encourage the whole group in its early stages. It is arguable that the WETA had so much going for it that the amount of time I have spent there was unjustified. But, apart from the fact that I think things would not have gone so well in some respects without my presence, there is also the consideration that I have learned a good deal from the project *because* the Association was managing well in any case. It has provided a useful contrast to my other main piece of work in the last few months with the teenagers in the Vernon Buildings tenement block.

A report, such as that given as an example here, should not be a final statement entirely, but a basis for further evaluation. A number of questions might be raised in relation to this or any other final report.

1. What were the values involved and how were these related to agency function?

   In the example given the worker implies but never very clearly states his own radical values, yet he was prepared to work closely with sections of the local authority. How far was this compromise worked out and how far was it the mere consequence of agency policy, itself a result of the need to maintain good relations with the Town Hall in order to retain grant aid?

2. What use was made of theory in the development of the worker's involvement?

   The worker indicates an awareness of theoretical work on community group development, but the setting of provisional objectives is not explicitly related to this theory in any way.

3. How far were the strategies adopted thought out, or did the worker make decisions for the short term which had, in fact, longer term implications?

   The worker, pursuing agency policy, encouraged the involvement of the Windmill Estate Tenants' Association in a federal structure without aparently assessing its possible impact on the Association (except in relation to the paper), though he does describe the effect in practice on the relationship between the chairman and secretary.

4. How far were all possible lines of action explored by the worker?

   Initial observations by the worker about vandalism on the estate and bad relations with the Riverbrook Estate seem to have resulted in no action by him, nor does he describe what happened to his original idea of setting up a handicraft group to make equipment for the playgroup.

5. What sort of relationship did the worker establish with the contact population?

There is a good deal of material in the report, but still some gaps. The worker speaks of himself as having been consciously a learner in the situation and one might ask how far this was made explicit to the contacts or how far he gave or attempted to give an impression of expertise that was not entirely justified.

6. What strengths and weaknesses did the worker exhibit in the project?

The worker has an evident tendency to make summary judgments of character, though he is also able to respond to people on closer contact. Contrast the relationships he made with Mrs Seabrook and Mr Smith on the one hand and Mr Loughton on the other.

7. What difference would it have made if the worker had not been involved?

This is in a sense the basic question the report should be an attempt to answer. But there are gaps in the example given. The worker is fairly clear on what he did contribute to the lunch club, playgroup and paper, not so clear on what he did not contribute to the Smith/Jones relationship, the problem of the hall and some of the other activities. If the group could handle the problems it did handle, could it have dealt with the problems that the worker handled? The answer does not have to be in the affirmative, but some kind of answer should be attempted.

Other types of recording

The discussion that has taken up most of this chapter has been concerned with the recording of 'projects', that is to say, units of work which, like 'cases', are relatively discrete in nature. This is far from being the only sort of recording necessary in community work, though it would probably be the central type. One of the functions of the community worker is to be a generalist with a wide range of knowledge that can be put at the disposal of community groups. He needs, like the caseworker, to be aware of a complex network of agencies, services, organisations and movements. For example, in the case of the WETA project, the worker Housing, Transport, Social Services and Education Departments, church authorities, a Women's Lib. Centre, a staff member at the local polytechnic, a local federation of community groups and probably many others besides. Apart from records on their own work, community workers need to maintain records on those agencies and networks and also need efficient cross-reference systems. The extent to which records of this type are needed depends, of course, on the nature of the agency and the need is more evident for multi-functional agencies covering wide areas. The imaginary agency used for the examples in this chapter was of this type and an instance of this sort of recording would be the detailed note the worker made on Social Services Department practice on lunch clubs when his work with the WETA incidentally gave him access to this general information. (See the record of the interview with Mrs Kelley, p. 92.) But while this form of general recording might be more useful for some agencies than others the principle that it is important is true of all types of agency.

Another point that might be made about recordings in community work settings is that written records are not necessarily the only kinds of record that are possible. Various visual forms such as maps, photographs, graphs and histograms and organisation charts might well be valuable in particular circumstances. Home movie films of social events, marches and other public happenings can also be instructive. Visual records can easily be more impressive than instructive but consideration of their use is something that should not be neglected.

Conclusion

The problems of recording in community work are considerable. There is not only the psychological disinclination to alter egalitarian relationships in subtle ways by recording them. There is also the fact that the basic unit of work in community work varies rather more considerably than it does in casework. Every caseworker has clients on whom records can focus. But the community worker may be dealing with a complex network of interlocking groups and not consider any one of them specifically as the 'client'. However, if community workers are to be serious about the work they do, then evaluation is necessary. This cannot be merely retrospective. It must also be part of the on-going process of work and written recording is important in ensuring that this is done. The importance of good recording is one of the respects in which community workers could have a good deal to learn from social work practice at its best.

9

Casework and community work

The general relationship between community work and social work

The relationship between caseworkers and community workers is problematic. This is because the boundary lines between them are unclear. Community workers and planners, to take one example, can get together, discuss, argue, disagree or agree, but the argument will be fairly clear-cut because it takes place between two quite separate groups who can, according to the values held by the participating individuals, define the extent to which they are enemies, allies, colleagues or friends. The problem between community workers and social workers is that many social workers, though themselves basically caseworkers, regard community work as part of the social work profession, while the majority of community workers appears to reject that assertion. This rejection is reinforced and rendered emotionally charged by the fact that most social workers are employed by local authorities and by the often misinformed and stereotyped pictures that community workers have of social work. It is further reinforced by the fact that community work as a part of the middle ground between social work and education (and to an even greater extent than other parts of that middle ground, such as youth work) has no obvious major group of employers and no establishment that belongs to it that has the power and authority to recognise courses leading to qualification in community work. With the best will in the world the social work profession has often tried in the recent past to make a contribution to community work training and practice, only to find this interpreted as a sinister and manipulative take-over bid.

Social workers have no reason to slow down developments in

their own training and practice which they see as relevant to their work and their clients' needs simply because this is likely to be interpreted in a paranoid way by some people. But any moves in this direction should not be based on the presupposition that community work is in some way a part of social work. Because it is not. I can personally see no reason in principle why it should not be. (Some community workers can. But I believe that that is a result of distorted impressions of social work.) In the United States community work is a recognised part of social work (Dunham, 1970) and had BASW not decided to exclude the Association of Community Workers from its constituent organisations when the new association for social workers was brought into existence, the same would have been true of this country. But professional identity is not something that derives from some platonic realm of ideas. It is an historical product. And the majority of community workers in this country just do not have social work as a primary reference point. It would, of course, be possible for the social work establishment to create a situation in which community work was officially regarded as a part of social work. (The major mechanism for this would presumably be the recognition of courses in straight community work by the Central Council for Education and Training in Social Work.) But the effect of this would be the emasculation of community work, not because of the malignant direct impact of social work on community workers, but because of the disaffection of a large number of present community workers that such a coercive measure would bring about. The result would be the loss of a great deal that has been gained since 1968.

The optimum development of community work in the next few years would probably be, like that of social work from the 1920s to the 1960s, in relation to different settings which would provide a framework in which skills and theory could be developed. One such setting is already well established—that of youth and community centre work under the umbrella of Local Education Authorities. Another that is developing is that of social work, in particular Social Services Departments, with the increasing community work content of generic social work courses. A third is that of urban management—and this would grow all the more quickly in the (unlikely) event of the government reversing previous decisions to shelve the Skeffington Report (1969). From work within these settings one might expect to see the eventual emergence of a semi-profession of community work, but it would be separate from (though, hopefully, working in close co-operation with) social work.

Community work and casework within social work settings

Unfortunately, the failures in communication between community workers and social workers have led to an over-emphasis on the ideologically-loaded general question of the relationship between the two semi-professions. This has meant a lack of serious thought about the relationship of casework and community work within social work settings.

One result of this has been the tendency of many community workers (and even disillusioned caseworkers, particularly those affected by the upheavals of Seebohmisation and local government re-organisation) to speak of community work as the radical alternative to casework. As long as people have problems which they cannot bring themselves to share with those normally close to them or with which they feel incapable of dealing, there will be a place for a service which helps them as individuals or as families. There is nothing intrinsically conservative about this. Community work itself can be conservative if it encourages the growth of some structures rather than others and a helping relationship with an individual can be established in a radical perspective in which client behaviour normally regarded as deviant and unacceptable is regarded as reasonable and acceptable by the worker. Sometimes the dubbing of all community work as 'radical' represents an abuse of the word 'radical' itself to mean anything outside normal procedure and routine.

The notion that community work is necessarily more radical than casework often goes with a notion that it is either cheaper or more effective. This is yet to be demonstrated. One sometimes comes across the thoughtless assumption that because a community worker is operating in an area with a population of a few thousand, then he is getting through to more people than a social caseworker with a caseload of forty or fifty. Merely stating this assumption baldly should be sufficient to bring out its absurdity. In practice the community worker himself is likely to have a 'caseload', so to speak, of only a few individuals with whom he is in frequent contact. The numbers could easily be fewer than those dealt with by the local authority social worker. Again, many of these may not be people with a wide range of pressing problems that are to some extent peculiar to themselves, but may merely share in the general problems of an area. The help that the community worker gives them may have a long-term effect which is arguably more important and beneficial than the patching up that is often done with casework clients because of pressure of work and circumstances. But the immediate pay-off (a playgroup or a better housing maintenance system, for example) may be trivial compared with the results of good casework with a number of families facing such problems as bereavement or eviction. Community work which involves having an individual or small team in a restricted area is particularly expensive and it is far harder to demonstrate its value in cost benefit terms to the contacts than good family casework.

Another false approach deriving more directly from seeing community work as the 'third method of social work' is to suggest that casework and community work run parallel to each other in a fairly simple way—the one dealing with individuals, the other with communities, the one with the unable, the other with the able. This was a view that was quite common among community workers in the 1960s and one can still hear echoes of it in Jones (1970). It was argued that community workers and caseworkers shared the same principles and objectives and that one could use social work terminology in a community work setting, so that the 'community' became the 'client' and one spoke of 'diagnosis', 'support' and so on in relation to community groups. The major difference was said to be that caseworkers dealt with the less able in any one grouping. Community workers who held this viewpoint were working mainly with fairly well-structured neighbourhood organisations, whose complexity did require certain skills and dispositions in their leaders. But it is inaccurate when applied generally and attempts to work in areas of extreme deprivation by seeking out the able and respectable have usually been disastrous because such people have been alien to the areas concerned. Very successful community work has been done with groups in which people who have been casework clients have assumed positions of leadership which they have managed perfectly well. Community action among and by highly deprived groups can be a means of producing radical improvements in self-estimation quite apart from any more specific gains (Potter, 1962). And, of course, many casework clients are not in any fundamental way unable and it would be contrary to casework principles to assume that, because they have come for help with a particular problem, they are generally incompetent.

Thinking based on catch-phrases about the 'three methods of

social work' has also led to attempts to define the situations in which casework, group work and community work are most appropriately chosen as the methods to be used (Tilbury, 1971). This is an awkward approach because the ways in which situations come to the attention of an agency, rather than the needs of the situation itself, often determine the form of work that must be undertaken in the first instance. It is no use telling a mother who comes for help with her children that help for her individual problems is beside the point because the real problem is the lack of play facilities in her locality. (This is not to deny that good casework might culminate in the mother taking the initiative in organising collective action to deal with that problem.)

A rather more useful approach was that suggested by Roché (1970) in an article that outlined what were charmingly called 'seven simple stages' in community work. These ranged from mobilising 'the community' in the interests of an individual or family in need through to the final stage of identifying 'growth buds' in the community and assisting in their 'flowering' and development. In other words, she attempted not to make a simple contrast, but to trace a connecting line between one aspect of casework and the third of the forms of community work identified by the Gulbenkian Group (Gulbenkian Study Group, 1968), taking in neighbourhood community development *en route* as her stage four. It is not evident that her stages flow into one another as smoothly as she suggests. But her approach does have the merit of illustrating how community work can be related to casework either in terms of the development of a basically casework service or in terms of a series of inter-connected agencies with related functions.

Accepting the usefulness of seeing the relationship in this way, but avoiding the precise classification of stages suggested by Roché, I would propose that the relationship might be seen in terms of five stages. Various other categorisations might, of course, be devised to bring out particular aspects of the issue.

The first stage would again be that of mobilising people outside the agency to help the client. A good deal of any social caseworker's time is spent in this way, in acting as an advocate to various other services or helping the client present his own case to them or in suggesting groups that the client might find it useful to join. As Roché says, 'It is still not sufficiently recognised that acquiring command of the map of society and cultivating relationships with workers on adjacent networks are essential skills in modern society.' Nor is this aspect of casework help merely concerned with formalised structures. The support (or its absence) of relatives, friends, neighbours and respected acquaintances can be crucial in helping people to cope with such problems as mental illness, terminal illness and mental handicap (Mills, 1962; Cartwright *et al.*, 1973; Bayley, 1973) and social workers need skills and opportunities to work with these networks. Whether one is talking about organised services or supportive networks, there is a *loose* sense in which any social caseworker is involved in community work as soon as he moves from a purely counselling role to one of involving others in helping his client.

The next stage would be to recognise this without reference to the needs of particular clients in the first instance. This might take the form of involving new sets of people in caring activity by establishing volunteer groups, or of structures designed to further inter-agency liaison (such as social workers' lunch clubs and social welfare forums). Again, this is work whose problems are often underestimated. Volunteers, for example, are too often seen as unpaid social workers or welfare assistants and then criticised for failing to fit in with such roles. It takes imagination for the professional members of a fully-stretched agency to appreciate the different types of function that may be suitable to different volunteers, their need to have their own mutual support system, the various sources of tension in their relationships with the professionals, or their value, not only as additional workers, but also as informed lay critics and as people able to spread social welfare values and understanding of stigmatised groups among the general public. There is a need, therefore, to recognise that work on inter-agency liaison or with volunteers or other activities that might come in this second stage is not a mere addition to the basic work load, but a step into a slightly new field, requiring new skills and understanding. Nevertheless, the type of community work that is involved here is still one that is strictly subordinate to the need of the agency to provide a good casework service. The scope of the work is restricted by a fairly narrow definition of the functions of the promoting agency. And the clients have not been actively involved.

A third stage would be to involve them actively, to start group work ventures in which the clients were given opportunities to help each other. This is already a form of work well known to many casework agencies in the form of prisoners' wives groups, clubs for the handicapped and so on. While it is well established, the quality of the work varies. Some social workers seem to suffer from a hang-up that work with groups must mean either psychotherapeutic group work of a highly skilled kind or simple socialising that involves the use of nothing more than common sense. Work with groups of clients that is not therapeutic except in a very vague sense still requires care and consideration. It is not a matter of common sense because the sense of what is normal group behaviour may not be common to the social workers and the clients concerned. Another problem is that as the clients of an agency have been brought together by that agency they may feel inhibited about assuming the initiative and they may well be right. It is not unknown for local authority social workers to create groups of foster parents to discuss problems, find that they are beginning to articulate grievances against the agency, unconsciously manipulate the group into a lack of self-confidence and then dissolution, and then blame the failure on the parents 'who did not know how to run things'. It is because of incidents of this sort that groups like Mothers In Action and Gingerbread are highly suspicious of attempts by social workers to start local branches of their movements. This is a type of work, therefore, that requires careful thought and definition of role and loyalties by the worker. Some community workers would dispute that it is community work. This would seem to reflect either a general suspicion of social workers or an exclusive concern with locality-based groups that results in an unrealistic attempt to draw boundaries. It seems reasonable to regard it as a form of community work and one that leads into the fourth stage.

This is the stage at which the worker stops concentrating on the clients as far as his community work planning is concerned. (This does not necessarily imply that he no longer has a caseload.) He might then help with group activities in which some clients are involved together with other people who are not clients but with whom they share problems and opportunities. For example, a social worker who had several clients sharing the same bad landlord might help all the tenants of that landlord form a Tenants' Association (Ballard, 1969). Or an agency which had several clients in an area might seize an opportunity to organise a community project in that area (Wardle, 1969). The initial stimulus to action may have been the fact that some of the clients had a problem in common, but gradually the focus of concern would shift to the collective activity itself.

The fifth stage would be to do 'pure' community work in which one's contacts with those one helped in collective action were not necessarily related at all to the functioning of a casework service. (This is not, incidentally, the same as Roché's seventh stage.) One might at that point question why a social work agency should sponsor such an activity and whether it might not be better organised from a specialist agency with a community work function.

'Stages', both those suggested here and those of Roché, could mean a number of things in practice. Each stage might be the primary function of a particular agency. Thus, taking my stages, the first might be undertaken by a casework agency, the second by a Council of Voluntary Service, the third by a specialist group work agency or by full-time workers employed by a federation of community groups, the fourth might be the work of a social-problem-oriented neighbourhood project and the fifth that of a general purpose community work agency. Alternatively, the stages might really be stages of development from a purely casework service to a casework service strengthened by an extension of activity into related fields by all the workers in the agency.

The stages include between them the forms of work which it was suggested in the first chapter might be undertaken by a Social Services Department—inter-agency liaison (stages one and two), organising volunteers (stage two), pre-school play (stage four), club work with the physically and mentally handicapped (stage three) and work with clients' organisations (stages three, four and five).

Social workers might have seen community work purely as a separate professional sphere of activity with which they needed to be in contact. This would have been welcomed by many community workers who are suspicious of social work and anxious to establish the separate identity of community work. But, quite rightly, the social work profession has seen that, in spite of all the strength of the one-to-one relationship as a basis for tackling problems, it cannot solve all the difficulties of clients and is impossible to maintain as the sole basis of work outside certain settings. The work of the social caseworker, unless he is very bad at his job, naturally spills over into the stages listed above as one to four. However many problems this causes for both social work and community work by fuzzing the boundaries of each and raising fears about group identity (in itself an interesting community work problem), this development is to be welcomed because it matches reality.

Individual problems arising in community work settings

The stages that were listed above were described in terms of attempts to deal with individual problems leading into involvement in collective activity. But this process might easily be reversed and a community worker may find himself faced with individual problems. This in itself raises a number of issues in relation to training and practice. The following situations illustrate some of the different ways in which individual problems can arise in relation to community work:

1. The community worker who has been assigned to a tenement block with a large proportion of elderly people comes across a number of individual problems relating to supplementary benefits and other services. By assisting people with these problems he establishes himself as a helpful and trustworthy person in the early stages of the project.

Here the worker by helping with individual problems lays the groundwork for his community work role to be accepted.

2. A man with a criminal record (for petty theft) offers his help in work on building an adventure playground. After some hesitation, his offer is accepted and by his substantial contribution to this phase of the project he rises in his own estimation and that of his neighbours.

Here involvement in collective activity contributes to the solving of one part of what had been regarded primarily as an individual problem.

3. A worker is involved in helping a group of parents in a highly deprived area to press for better play facilities. The parents themselves are apathetic until the accidental death of a child playing on the road generates first anger and then a willingness to undertake action. The bereaved mother and her dead child are made a sort of symbol for the campaign. The mother is interviewed on television, etc.

Here an individual and a collective problem are inextricably involved with one another. The difficulty would be to use the movement that has been created by the incident without exploiting the parents concerned.

4. A couple involved in a community project approach the community worker with an admission that they have marital difficulties and a request to the worker to help in this. When the worker suggests that they go to Marriage Guidance for help they react

negatively, suggesting that they do not want to be labelled as having a marital problem and that the community worker is ideal as someone who is both a friend and an outsider.

This is the reverse of situation 1. The main difficulties would arise from the worker's possible lack of competence to deal with this sort of situation. Even if he were competent, there might be a role conflict between his main community worker role and the proposed counselling role.

5. A small group of teenagers who appear to be isolated in various ways from the existing networks of their peers in their locality have begun to form a social group around a neighbourhood worker. They are joined and disrupted by a newcomer whose problems appear to be more drastic than theirs and who tries, among other things, to push 'speed' in the group.

This is in some ways a reverse of situation 2. Someone with problems is not helped by but is threatening a community group. A major question of principle would arise here of whether the priority was the group or the member most in need. Goetschius (1969) in his numerous references to 'socio-pathic leadership' suggests that it should be the group, but not all would agree with him. A good deal depends on the type of group concerned and, besides, it is one thing to put the group first in principle and another to reject an actual person who is dangerous to the group. There is a fascinating detailed case study of a similar problem arising over a bingo group in Twelvetrees (1974).

6. A middle-aged woman from a working-class area has become involved in a neighbourhood organisation and through that with a wider federal structure. This experience has taught her that her skills and talents are greater than she had realised and she is acquiring ambitions and social contacts that take her outside her original environment. This in turn causes stress between her and her husband and children. It brings into the open problems in her marriage. She is unable to make a straight-forward break and her ambivalence also begins to affect her contribution to her neighbourhood organisation.

Here again there is a sort of reverse of situation 2. The community work project actually causes the individual problem. There is also an issue of values because the 'problem' has some positive aspects. The woman is discovering strengths she did not realise she had. She is re-examining a relationship which has had a number of negative aspects. There is also a problem of role conflict similar to that in situation 4. To what extent is it either legitimate or practicable for the worker to offer help with this personal problem when there is no explicit request for it but may be an implicit request in that the woman talks about it?

While not exactly typical, such situations are not uncommon in community work practice and they raise questions about the need for skills in handling personal problems for those engaged in community work. On the basis of situations such as these some people have suggested that some training in casework would be useful for all community workers. But the matter is more difficult than that. One cannot simply equate dealing with individual problems with casework.

In situation 1 casework skills would be very useful, though they might be at a fairly simple level. In situation 4 experience in marital casework might be highly useful. But in situation 6 it might be a positive handicap in a less sensitive worker since he might unconsciously move into a type of counselling role that was not wanted by the woman concerned. A similar consideration applies to situation 2 where the 'therapy' would be likely to work precisely to the extent that the label of 'criminal' was forgotten by the others concerned. In situation 5, assuming that the worker wished to help the particularly deviant teenager and that there were indications that he wished to be helped, it would not be possible to detach him neatly from the group. Any help would, therefore, have to be given within the group situation and skills developed in working in one-to-one relationships would be of limited relevance. Situation 3 is the most complicated since the group both shares and does not share in the problem of the bereaved parents. At best the campaign might prove a highly constructive piece of 'grief-work', producing a spin-off for the children in the locality as well as helping the bereaved parents. At worst the fact that the dead child had become a group symbol might make it difficult for the parents to come to terms with the death of the real and not symbolic child and expose them to forms of emotional strain without giving them compensating support. The skills involved in dealing with an incident of this sort would not normally form a central part of the teaching material on either community work or social work courses. Normal approaches to the problems of campaign organisation and normal approaches to bereavement counselling would both be of limited, though real, relevance.

In general the sort of questions raised by the situations described above have not been given much consideration except to some extent on youth and community work courses. The work situations concerned are different from those to which most social workers are accustomed. The focus of concern is different to that most community workers share.

Structural relationships between caseworkers and community workers in social work settings

If casework and community work spill over into each other then no clear boundaries can be drawn in practice. But boundaries may need to be roughly drawn because disciplined work demands that the worker have a focus for his activity. Specifically, if community work is to be done within a social work agency, then the relationship between casework and community work in that agency has to be defined in structural terms.

If the agency acts on the assumption that community work is going to be part of the normal function of all its social workers, a number of things follow. The administrative structure has to allow for this to happen. The greater the decentralisation of the agency, unless it is very small to begin with, the easier it will be. If each basic grade social worker has his geographical patch from which at least most of his cases come, then he is more likely to pick up on aspects of the area that will enable him to promote collective activity. Another requirement would be that caseloads were lighter than they are at present in many agencies.

To meet these conditions many social work agencies would have to change (though often in terms of going further in directions already taken). This and the fact that the making of community work a normal function of social workers would have radical implications for the courses leading to the Certificate of Qualifications in Social Work might suggest that it would be preferable to have specialist community workers within the agency.

Such a conclusion should not be reached too hastily. As was argued earlier, casework naturally spills over into community work. It is not certain, moreover, that it would necessarily be a good thing to have a large number of 'generic' community workers in social work agencies. The more community work that is done by people in such professional fields as social work, medicine, education and planning, the better, provided that it is done well. It would be especially dangerous if a majority of the specialist community workers were to be concentrated in social work agencies as this might distract attention from the openings for community work in other settings.

There are, in fact, a number of problems that arise if specialist community workers are employed by social work agencies which are basically operating casework services. These all focus on the strong possibility of a mutual misunderstanding about the community worker's role and style of work. In the days of the community work bandwagon that followed the publication of the Gulbenkian and Seebohm Reports too many social work agencies appeared to appoint community workers without making clear to themselves or the workers what they expected their role to be. Administrative structures are also important here. Some of the points made early in chapter 3 about agency setting and the effect that different administrative structures can have on the community worker's freedom of operation are particularly relevant to Social Services Departments. And, whatever arrangements are made in this respect, there will need to be a plan to educate both case-workers and community workers about each other's roles.

Conclusion

Most people will hope that issues of this sort will soon be as well resolved as can reasonably be expected and that social work will make a valuable contribution to the development of community work in this country as it has in others. It has many of the means to do so. Social workers have access to resources, they are in touch with crucial social problems of all sorts and they have established forms of training and education which, with their emphasis on analysing situations, planning of work and integration of theory and practice, offer a good deal in the way of models to community workers. If community workers can learn to make use of the achievements of social work and if social workers can learn from community workers to see a new dimension to their role, then a major contribution will have been made to discovering new ways in which people can be helped to create a society that is more democratic and more caring than the one we have at present.

Further reading

The bi-monthly publication *Community Action* (7a Frederick Mews, Kinnerton Street, London SW1) has many news items on community group activities and excellent guides to technical and legal matters. It is absolutely indispensable for anyone taking a serious interest in community work and action. The *Community Development Journal* (Oxford University Press) is another specialist publication. Both *Social Work Today* and the *British Journal of Social Work* have frequently published articles on community work and for relevant aspects of social administration it is useful to read *Planning, Housing* and *Housing Review*.

In 1974 Routledge & Kegan Paul began publication of an annual collection of articles on community work in co-operation with the Association of Community Workers (Jones and Mayo, 1974).

Community work and action are for obvious reasons in some respects more amenable to film than casework. This is not always an advantage as visual interest can push out intelligent description. But there are a number of useful TV and film documentaries available.

Chapter 1

The best introductions to the British scene are Gulbenkian Study Group (1968) and Community Work Study (1973). For the American scene by way of comparison: Dunham (1970); for community work in a social work setting: Seebohm (1968), in adult education settings: Clyne (1974) and in youth work settings: Youth Service Development Council (1969).

Chapter 2

Cheetham and Hill (1973) is a good starting point.

Chapter 3

No-one could feel happy about suggesting a few books to cover all the themes mentioned in this chapter, but on aspects of social administration not normally covered in social work courses: Tetlow and Goss (1968), Cullingworth (1972), Donnison (1973); on local politics: Bealey *et al.* (1965), Hampton (1970), Jones (1969); on social movements: McLaughlin (1969); on community structures: Frankenberg (1966); on neighbourhood interaction: Keller (1968).

Chapter 4

Biddle and Biddle (1965) and Goetschius (1969) are useful on the community development process, but fairly conservative. There is no good general book on radical community work in this country and even case studies tend to be goodies *vs* baddies epics with little analysis. Exceptions include Popplestone (1972). One very good book on work with a particular type of community group is Crowe (1973).

The novel tends to focus on individuals and few are useful for their imaginative reconstructions of social movements. The notable exception is Zola's *Germinal* (available in Penguin and Everyman editions). In a lighter vein there is the latter half of Robert Heinlein's science-fiction story *Red Planet* (Pan Books).

Chapter 5

For comparisons see the chapters in Dunham (1958) and Community Work Group (1973).

Chapter 6

The articles cited in the text are the most useful source. See also Lippitt *et al.* (1958).

Bibliography

ALINSKY, S. (1969), *Reveille for Radicals*, Random House.

ARGYLE, M. (1967), *The Psychology of Interpersonal Behaviour*, Penguin.

ARNSTEIN, S. R. (1969), 'A Ladder of Citizen Participation', *Journal of the American Institute of Planners*, 35.

BAILEY, R. (1972), *The Squatters*, Penguin.

BALLARD, R. (1969), 'Social Action and the Local Authority Social Worker', *Case Conference*, 16, no. 5.

BANKS, J. A. (1972), *The Sociology of Social Movements*, Macmillan.

BARR, A. (1972), *Student Community Action*, National Council of Social Service.

BATTEN, T. R. (1967), *The Non-directive Approach to Group and Community Work*, Oxford University Press.

BAYLEY, M. (1973), *Mental Handicap and Community Care*, Routledge & Kegan Paul.

BEALEY, F. et al. (1965), *Constituency Politics: A Study of Newcastle-under-Lyme*, Faber & Faber.

BEDDINGTON, N. (1972), 'Community Newspapers and how to start them', *Community Action*, 3.

BENNINGTON, J. (1972), 'Community Work as an Instrument of Institutional Change' in *Lessons From Experience*, Report of the 1972 Annual Conference of the Association of Community Workers.

BERNSTEIN, S. (1960), 'Self-determination: King or Citizen in the Realm of Values?' *Social Work*, 5, no. 1.

BIDDLE, W. W. and BIDDLE, L. J. (1965), *The Community Development Process: The Rediscovery of Local Initiative*, Holt, Rinehart & Winston.

BODINGTON, S. (1973), *Neighbourhood Councils and Modern Technology*, Spokesman Pamphlet no. 28, Bertrand Russell Peace Foundation.

BOND, N. (1972), *The Hillfields Information and Opinion Centre: The Evolution of a Social Agency Controlled by Local Residents*, Coventry CDP Occasional Paper, no. 2.

BOOKER, I. (1960), 'Western Siciliy: A Problem for Community Development', *Social Services Quarterly*, 34, no. 2.

BIBLIOGRAPHY

BOOKER, I. (1962), 'Project in Menfi: An Experiment in Social Development', *Social Services Quarterly*, 35, no. 4.

BORLEY, R. (1972), 'Community Work in the Local Authority', *Social Work Today*, 3, no. 6.

BOTTOMORE, T. B. and RUBEL, M. (eds) (1963), *Karl Marx: Selected Writings in Sociology and Social Philosophy*, C. A. Watts.

BRACEY, H. E. (1964), *Neighbours*, Routledge & Kegan Paul.

BRASNETT, M. (1964), *The Story of the Citizens Advice Bureaux*, National Council of Social Service.

BRASNETT, M. (1969), *Voluntary Social Action: A History of the National Council of Social Service 1919-1969*, National Council of Social Service.

BRIER, A. P. and DOWSE, R. E. (1966), 'The Amateur Activists', *New Society*, 222.

BROOKE, R. (1972), *Information and Advice Services*, Occasional Papers on Social Administration, no. 46.

BRYANT, R. (1972), 'Community Action', *British Journal of Social Work*, 2, no. 3.

BRYANT, R. (1974), 'Linking Community and Industrial Action' *Community Development Journal*, 9, no. 1.

CARTWRIGHT, A. *et al.* (1973), *Life Before Death*, Routledge & Kegan Paul.

CENTRE FOR URBAN STUDIES (1964), 'Tall Flats in Pimlico' in *London: Aspects of Change*, Centre for Urban Studies, MacGibbon & Kee.

CHEESEMAN, D. *et al.* (1972), *Neighbourhood Care and Old People: A Community Development Project*, National Council of Social Service.

CHEETHAM, J. and HILL, M. S. (1973), 'Community Work: Social Realities and Ethical Dilemmas', *British Journal of Social Work*, 3, no. 3.

CHOMBART DE LAUWE, P. (1959/60), *Famille et Habitation* 2 vols., Centre National de la Recherche Scientifique, Paris.

CLARK, D. B. (1973), 'The Concept of Community: A Re-examination', *Sociological Review*, 21, no. 3.

CLYNE, P. (1974), *The Disadvantaged Adult*, Longman.

COLLISON, P. (1963), *The Cutteslowe Walls: A Study of Social Class*, Faber & Faber.

COMMUNITY ACTION (1972), 'The Urban Aid Programme', *Community Action*, 3.

COMMUNITY WORK GROUP (1973), *Current Issues in Community Work*, Routledge & Kegan Paul.

COSER, L. A. (1954), *The Functions of Social Conflict*, Free Press.

COX, H. (1965), *The Secular City*, Student Christian Movement Press.

CROWE, B. (1973), *The Playgroup Movement*, Allen & Unwin.

CULLINGWORTH, J. B. (1972), *Town and Country Planning in Britain* (rev. ed.), Allen & Unwin.

CURRAMS, R. (1971), 'What Community Development Presupposes', *Social Work Today*, 2, no. 16.

DAVIES, J. C. (1962), 'Toward a Theory of Revolution', *American Sociological Review*, 27.

DEMERATH, N. J. and PETERSON, R. A. (eds) (1967), *System, Change and*

Conflict, Collier-Macmillan.

DEMERS, J. F. (1962), 'Social Work in Housing', *Social Services Quarterly*, 36, no. 2.

DEMERS, J. F. (1972), 'Community Development in a British New Town', *Community Development Journal*, 7, no. 2.

DENNIS, N. (1958), 'The Popularity of the Neighbourhood/Community Idea', *Sociological Review*, n.s. 6.

DENNIS, N. (1961), 'Changes in Function and Leadership Renewal', *Sociological Review*, 9, no. 1.

DEUTSCH, M. (1969), 'Conflicts: Productive and Destructive', *Journal of Social Issues*, 25, no. 1.

DICKSON, M. and DICKSON, A. (1967), *Count Us In: A Community Service Handbook*, Dobson.

DONNISON, D. (1973), 'What is the "Good City"?', *New Society*, 584.

DUNHAM, A. (1958), *Community Welfare Organisation: Principles and Practice*, Thomas Y. Cromwell.

DUNHAM, A. (1970), *The New Community Organisation*, Thomas Y. Crowell.

DURANT, R. (1939), *Watling: A Survey of Social Life on a New Housing Estate*, King.

EASTON, P. (1968), 'Community Transport', *Social Services Quarterly*, 42, no. 1.

ELIAS, N. and SCOTSON, J. L. (1965), *The Established and the Outsiders*, Frank Cass.

EPSTEIN, I. (1970), 'Professionalisation, Professionalism and Social Worker Radicalism', *Journal of Health and Social Behaviour*, March.

ETZIONI, A. (1968), *The Active Society*, Free Press.

FELLIN, P. and LITWAK, E. (1963), 'Neighbourhood Cohesion under Conditions of Mobility', *American Sociological Review*, 28, no. 3.

FERGUSON, J. (1974), 'Report on the Volunteer Bureau' in Ferguson, J. and McGlone, P., *Towards Voluntary Action*, Manchester Council of Voluntary Service.

FERRIS, J. (1972), *The Barnsbury Affair*, Occasional Papers in Social Administration, no. 48.

FESTINGER, L. and KELLEY, H. H. (1951), *Changing Attitudes Through Social Contact*, Ann Arbor.

FEUER, L. J. (ed.) (1959), *Marx and Engels: Basic Writings on Politics and Philosophy*, Anchor Books, Doubleday.

FRANKENBERG, R. (1966), *Communities in Britain*, Penguin.

FREEDMAN, R. (ed.) (1968), *Marxist Social Thought*, Harcourt, Brace & World.

FREEMAN, J. (1973), *The Tyranny of Structurelessness*, pamphlet issued by Leeds Women's Organisation of Revolutionary Anarchists.

FRITH, D. (1972), 'Claimants' Unions', *Social Work Today*, 3, no. 5.

GIBB, C. A. (ed.) (1969), *Leadership*, Penguin.

GODSCHALK, D. R. (1972), *Participation, Planning and Exchange in Old and New Communities*, Centre for Urban and Regional Studies, University of North Carolina.

GOETSCHIUS, G. W. (1969), *Working with Community Groups: Using*

Community Development as a Method of Social Work, Routledge & Kegan Paul.

GOULDNER, A. W. (1955), *Wildcat Strike: A Study of an Unofficial Strike*, Routledge & Kegan Paul.

GREVE, J. (1973), 'The British Community Development Project—some interim comments', *Community Development Journal*, 8, no. 3.

GULBENKIAN STUDY GROUP (1968), *Community Work and Social Change*, Longman.

GURVITCH, G. (1950), *La Vocation actuelle de la sociologie*, Presses Universitaires de France.

GUSFIELD, J. R. (1966), 'Functional Areas of Leadership in Social Movements', *Sociological Quarterly*, 7, no. 2.

HALSEY, A. H. (1974), 'Government against Poverty in School and Community' in Wedderburn, D. (ed.), *Poverty, Inequality and Class Structure*, Cambridge University Press.

HAMPTON, W. (1970), *Democracy and Community: A Study of Politics in Sheffield*, Oxford University Press.

HARE, A. P. (1962), *Handbook of Small Group Research*, Free Press.

INGLIS, K. S. (1963), *Churches and the Working Classes in Victorian England*, Routledge & Kegan Paul.

INSTITUT DE SOCIOLOGIE URBAINE (1968), *Travaux de l'Institut de Sociologie Urbaine*, special edition of *Revue Française de Sociologie*, 9, no. 2.

ISAJIW, W. W. (1968), *Causation and Functionalism in Sociology*, Routledge & Kegan Paul.

JAY, A. (1972), *The Householder's Guide to Community Defence Against Bureaucratic Oppression*, Jonathan Cape.

JENNINGS, H. (1962), *Societies in the Making: A Study of Development and Redevelopment within a County Borough*, Routledge & Kegan Paul.

JOHANN, R. O. (1970), 'Developing Community', *The Way*, 10, no. 2.

JONES, D. and MAYO, M. (eds) (1974), *Community Work: One*, Routledge & Kegan Paul.

JONES, G. W. (1969), *Borough Politics: A Study of Wolverhampton Town Council 1888-1964*, Macmillan.

JONES, K. (1970), 'Casework and Community Work', *Social Work Today*, 1, no. 8.

JORDAN, W. (1973), *Paupers: The Making of a New Claiming Class*, Routledge & Kegan Paul.

KELLER, S. (1968), *The Urban Neighbourhood: A Sociological Perspective*, Random House.

LEAPER, R. (1971), *Community Work: An Introduction*, National Council of Social Service.

LIPPITT, R. et al. (1958), *The Dynamics of Planned Change: A Comparative Study of Principles and Techniques*, Harcourt, Brace & World.

LITWAK, E. (1960), 'Reference Group Theory: Bureaucratic Career and Neighbourhood Primary Group Cohesion', *Sociometry*, 23.

LITWAK, E. (1961), 'Voluntary Associations and Neighbourhood Cohesion', *American Sociological Review*, 26, no. 2.

LITWAK, E. and SZELENYI, I. (1969), 'Primary Group Structures and their Functions: Kin, Neighbours and Friends', *American Sociological Review*, 34, no. 4.

MANN, P. N. (1965), *An Approach to Urban Sociology*, Routledge & Kegan Paul.

MCGLONE, P. (1974), 'Report on the Care Scheme Project' in Ferguson, J. and McGlone, P. *Towards Voluntary Action*, Manchester Council of Voluntary Service.

MCLAUGHLIN, B. (ed) (1969), *Studies in Social Movements: A Social Psychological Perspective*, Free Press.

MELLOR, W. H. (1951), 'The Function of the Community Association', *Sociological Review*, 43.

MILLER, J. (1973), 'Community Development in a Disaster Community', *Community Development Journal*, 8, no. 3.

MILLS, E. (1962), *Living with Mental Illness*, Routledge & Kegan Paul.

MILLS, T. M. (1965), 'Some Hypotheses on Small Groups from Simmel' in Coser, L. A. (ed.), *The Makers of Modern Social Science: Georg Simmel*, Prentice-Hall.

MITCHELL, G. D. *et al.* (1954), *Neighbourhood and Community*, Liverpool University Press.

MITTON, R. and MORRISON, E. (1972), *A Community Project in Notting Dale*, Allen Lane.

MOGEY, J. M. (1956), *Family and Neighbourhood: Two Studies in Oxford*, Oxford University Press.

MORRIS, R. N. and MOGEY, J. M. (1965), *The Sociology of Housing: Studies at Berinsfield*, Routledge & Kegan Paul.

PARK, R. E. (1952), *Human Communities: The City and Human Ecology*, Collected Papers Vol. 2, Free Press.

PATEMAN, C. (1970), *Participation and Democratic Theory*, Cambridge University Press.

PLANT, R. (1969), *Social and Moral Theory in Casework*, Routledge & Kegan Paul.

POPPLESTONE, G. (1971), 'The Ideology of the Professional Community Workers', *British Journal of Social Work*, 1, no. 1.

POPPLESTONE, G. (1972), 'Collective Action Among Private Tenants', *British Journal of Social Work*, 2, no. 3.

POTTER, R. (1962), *Homeless! Halfway House Tenants Speak Out*, Solidarity Pamphlet no. 12.

POWER, A. (1972), 'Neighbourhood Groups in Islington' in *Lessons From Experience*, Report of the Annual Conference of the Association of Community Workers.

REX, J. and MOORE, R. (1967), *Race, Community and Conflict: A Study of Sparkbrook*, Oxford University Press.

RICHES, G. (1973), 'Rethinking the Role of a Settlement', *Social Work Today*, 4, no. 15.

ROCHÉ, E. (1970), 'Guide to Community Work in Seven Simple Stages', *Social Work Today*, 1, no. 11.

ROSE, H. (1973), 'Up Against the Welfare State: The Claimants' Union Movement', in Millibrand, R. and Saville, J. (eds), *Socialist Register*

1973, Merlin.

RUNCIMAN, W. G. (1966), *Relative Deprivation and Social Justice*, Routledge & Kegan Paul.

SEEBOHM (1968), *Report of the Committee on Local Authority and Allied Personal Social Services*, HMSO.

SHELTER (1972), *The New Granby Centre and SNAP Liverpool*, Shelter.

SIMMEL, G. (1971), *On Individuality and Social Forms*, ed. Levine, D. N., University of Chicago Press.

SKEFFINGTON (1969), *People and Planning: The Report of the Committee on Public Participation in Planning*, HMSO.

SKELTON, P. and SIMPSON, D. (1972), 'Credit Unions', *Community Action*, 4.

SKIPPER, J. (1969), *Out into the Community*, Sheffield Council of Social Service.

SMITH, C. et al. (1972), *The Wincroft Youth Project: A Social Work Programme in a Slum Area*, Tavistock.

SPENCER, J. (1964), *Stress and Release in an Urban Housing Estate*, Tavistock.

TETLOW, J. and GOSS, A. (1968), *Homes, Towns and Traffic*, Faber & Faber.

THOMASON, G. F. (1969), *The Professional Approach to Community Work*, Sands.

TILBURY, D. (1971), 'Selection of Method in Social Work', *Social Work Today*, 2, no. 2.

TURNER, N. (1973), *Community Radio in Britain: A Practical Introduction*, Whole Earth Tools Inc.

TUROWSKI, J. (1968), 'The Problem of the Local Community in the Big City', *Polish Sociological Bulletin*, 18, no. 2.

TWELVETREES, A. C. (1971), 'An Explanatory Study of Community Associations Based on Four Areas of Edinburgh', *International Review of Community Development*, nos 25-6, Rome.

TWELVETREES, A. C. (1974), *The Braunstone Neighbourhood Project: The First Six Years*, Leicester Family Service Unit.

WARDLE, M. (1969), 'The Lordsville Project', *Case Conference*, 16, no. 11.

WERTHEIM, W. F. (1974), *Evolution and Revolution*, Penguin.

WESTERGAARD, J. (1965), 'The Withering Away of Class: A Contemporary Myth', in Anderson, P. and Blackburn, R. (eds), *Towards Socialism*, Collins.

WHITE, L. (1950), *Community or Chaos?*, National Council of Social Service.

W.L., LIVERPOOL (1973), 'Power to Control', *Community Action*, 8.

WOOLEY, T. (1972), *Community Action: The Politics of Intervention*, Solidarity Pamphlet.

WORSLEY, P. et al. (1970), *Introducing Sociology*, Penguin.

YOUTH SERVICE DEVELOPMENT COUNCIL (1969), *Youth and Community Work in the 1970s*, HMSO.